SEDONA

PSYCHIC ENERGY VORTEXES

ALSO BY DICK SUTPHEN

Soul Agreements

Wisdom Erases Karma

*You Were Born Again to Be Together**

*Available from Hay House
Please visit:

Hay House USA: www.hayhouse.com®
Hay House Australia: www.hayhouse.com.au
Hay House UK: www.hayhouse.co.uk
Hay House India: www.hayhouse.co.in

SEDONA

PSYCHIC ENERGY VORTEXES

TRUE STORIES OF HEALING
AND TRANSFORMATION FROM
ONE OF THE WORLD'S MOST
POWERFUL ENERGY CENTERS

DICK SUTPHEN

HAY HOUSE, INC.
Carlsbad, California • New York City
London • Sydney • New Delhi

Published in the United States by: Hay House, Inc.: www.hayhouse.com®
Published in Australia by: Hay House Australia Pty. Ltd.: www.hayhouse.com.au • *Published in the United Kingdom by:* Hay House UK, Ltd.: www.hayhouse.co.uk • *Published in India by:* Hay House Publishers India: www.hayhouse.co.in

Cover design: Julie Davison
Interior design: Nick C. Welch
Interior illustrations: Dick Sutphen

Library of Congress Card Number for the Original Edition: 86-050562

Cataloging-in-Publication Data is on file at the Library of Congress.

Tradepaper ISBN: 978-1-4019-6682-9
E-book ISBN: 978-1-4019-6683-6
Audiobook ISBN: 978-1-4019-6684-3

10 9 8 7 6 5 4 3 2 1
1st edition, 1986
1st Hay House edition, April 2022

Printed in the United States of America

SUSTAINABLE FORESTRY INITIATIVE
Certified Chain of Custody
Promoting Sustainable Forestry
www.sfiprogram.org
SFI-01268
SFI label applies to the text stock

CONTENTS

FOREWORD

There is no place on earth like Sedona, with its majestic red rocks and awe-inspiring beauty. This mystical desert beckons you as soon as it comes into view. And there is no better teacher than the late Dick Sutphen to take you on such a rich exploration of this unusual and compelling place.

I spent more than five years living and working in Sedona, and have held numerous psychic workshops in the area. As someone who has dedicated her life as an intuitive and psychic medium, I can unequivocally say everything in this book is true. You will just need an open mind to let it all in.

There is *real* magic in Sedona.

In the first chapter of this book, Dick talks about the phenomenon of *psychic migration*, which perfectly illustrates how I, too, was called to Sedona. My husband and I were living in Canada at the time. I was a new author at Hay House, and after a speaking event in Las Vegas, my husband and I spontaneously decided to go to Sedona. Neither of us had been there, although I had been having powerful dreams of the red rocks and the canyons. I knew I was drawn there. We went for a holiday adventure, and as we entered the town, I felt something so intense. Looking back, I liken it now to a super strength magnetic tractor beam, telling me to be there, to live there—to pack up and move there. It was the strangest feeling, and I couldn't shake it.

There was some purpose for us to be there, although I had no idea what it was. Sedona is remote—roughly two hours away from the Phoenix airport—and we were Canadian citizens, so we could not just up and move there! But I could not get it out of my mind. We visited some of the vortexes and I had a number of elevated experiences meditating, similar to an experience I had in Glastonbury, England, another sacred place. I kept seeing the terrain the way it was without the houses, the way it was in its original form, in my peripheral vision. I also was struck by the emotional intensity of Sedona. Everything was exaggerated. As a psychic medium, I expected to experience something, but not to the extent I did. I knew I was on some kind of energy grid, without knowing anything specific. I could see waves wafting over the land, like a ribbon of electricity, of a life force that wasn't like anything I had ever experienced or could put language to.

After our first visit, which in retrospect was more like an initiation, we returned to Canada and within months, against all odds, we had US visas that enabled us to move.

Just like that, we took our place with the many people from all over the world who would say the very same things when asked how they came to live in Sedona: "I don't know why I came, I was called here." "I just knew I had to come." "I came once then knew I had to come back to live." The psychic migration is a collective calling and comes with a hefty price tag. You must do your inner work, face your shadows, and be of service, or you will watch the red rocks remove all that doesn't work in your life without your consent. The challenge is real. Everyone who has ever lived there knows this well.

I came to understand each vortex was different, like they had their own purpose, even their own personalities. For example, a meditation at Bell Rock, my favorite hiking vortex, was vastly different from Boynton Canyon. Bell Rock was electric yet soft, grounded and often hopeful, whereas Boynton Canyon always felt serious, challenging, and all encompassing. We lived very close to Cathedral Rock, where the energy was feminine, creative, and strong yet flexible. I really understood the nature of channeling while living there. I completed my book *Messages from Spirit* in Sedona; my oracle deck *Wisdom of the Hidden Realms* came as a result of a series of dreams I had there; and my book *The Map* was incubated there, too. Sedona made me a prolific writer and creator. I felt its magic weave its way through me every day. Sedona truly has a purpose, a destiny for each person called there.

We all come to be changed, to be healed, and then sharpened in some way through the seductive mystery of this place. Sedona's powerful energy is like being inside a cosmic vibration upgrade, both brilliant and enlightening and wildly disruptive. There's a saying, *Sedona will draw you in, then when she is finished with you, she'll spit you out*, and it is more than true. I loved it there until the day it was time to move on. I am always grateful for the experience there. Back in Canada now, Sedona still reaches into my spirit once in a while and my heart remembers.

On a recent visit, I stood in line at one of the local grocery stores, and I was struck by the synchronicities. As I overheard their conversations I wondered about the spiritual adventure calling each person that I observed standing there, in urgent and meaningful conversation, as I once did. I was amazed at how and why they got there.

Take a trip to Sedona with this book as your guide. I guarantee something magical is awaiting you.

Colette Baron-Reid

INTRODUCTION
TO THE VORTEXES

Sedona, Arizona—a place of awesome beauty and an extraordinary energy that is felt by every person wandering through its red-rock canyons. The first time I saw Sedona, in 1969, I knew this was a special place, not only because of its magnificent beauty but because of an undeniable spiritual vibration emanating throughout the area. Over the years I've become convinced, through my own experiences and the experiences of others, and through extensive research and investigation, that the psychic energy here is greater than anywhere else in the country.

The explanation for this may come from a book called *The Romeo Error* by biologist Lyall Watson. The following is a quote from that book:

> Navigation is bedeviled by the fact that the earth's magnetic field is riddled with local deviations and irregularities. These faults have been very carefully plotted and the most persistent of them have become quite notorious. One of these lies off the Bahama Islands (the Bermuda Triangle), another in the English county of Sussex, and a third near Prescott in Arizona.[1]

What Watson is describing is a vortex—a positive or negative "power spot"—where a great concentration of energy emits from the earth. Positive vortexes expand and perpetuate energy; negative vortexes dissipate energy.

There are many vortexes on earth, and a good analogy might be to compare them to the acupressure points on the human body. Although there are many vortexes, there are very few major vortex areas; Watson's above quote pinpoints the one "near Prescott" as one of those.

Prescott and Sedona are only about 30 miles apart as the crow flies (60 miles by car over the mountains). After considerable investigation, with the assistance of many psychically oriented individuals, I have concluded that it is the Sedona vortexes of which Watson writes.

It also appears that Sedona is considered one of the major vortex areas, not because of one vortex but because of the four powerful vortexes within a few square miles of each other. In fact, there are more vortexes concentrated in Sedona than in any other area on earth. This probably explains the intense psychic vibrations in the entire area.

I first wrote about Sedona in my book *Past Lives, Future Loves*, which was published by Simon & Schuster Pocket Books in 1978. In it, I related the results of some library research that had unearthed the following information from *Sedona Life* magazine, "Religion of the Red Mountains" by Heather Hughes:

> [L]egend tells us that there are four places in the world designated as "power spots" and that these four are broken into two plus two—two positive and two negative, or two "light" and two "dark." It is believed that the two "positive" places in the world are Kauai, an island in Hawaii, and Sedona, both red-rock country. Sedona and Kauai are vortexes of energy in which the Great Spirit gives birth to rainbows.

[American] Indians tell us that the towering crimson peaks stimulate sensitivity and that here a man realizes his true dreams and ambitions. They also say that the mountains are like a great magnet and that people are drawn to them because it is the home of the Great Spirit. Amid red-rock country, it is said that man comes face to face with himself and the potentials of his nature.[2]

And from my own observations and experiences, I believe this to be true. For that reason, in April of 1983, I conducted my first psychic seminar in Sedona. Because of Sedona's incredible energy and the effects which I, as well as others, had experienced there, I felt it would be the ideal place to conduct seminars in which individuals could learn to tap into and develop the psychic potentials within themselves that we all possess to one degree or another. The results were incredible!

Although Sedona was named after pioneer woman Sedona Schnebly, a Sedona Psychic Seminar participant noticed what may be a cosmic joke: the name Sedona spelled backward is "anodes," a term relating to electrical current.

Usually, as part of my Sedona Psychic Seminars, the participants visit one or more of the energy vortexes. Positive vortexes are charged in one of three ways, according to psychic Page Bryant:

- **Electric:** These are "yang," charged with the male force. When you enter the vibrational field or frequency, you will become charged emotionally and physically. The energy will stimulate and elevate consciousness. It is also ideal to eliminate depression. Some people, however, consider an electrical vortex to be a strain on someone with high blood pressure or heart problems.

- **Magnetic**: These are "yin," charged with the female force. When you enter the vibrational field or frequency, you can expect to open psychically, becoming much more perceptive, for the area primarily affects the subconscious mind.

- **Electromagnetic**: These vortexes are a combination of electrical and magnetic, or a combination of the yin [and] yang forces, resulting in a perfect state of balance. When you enter the vibrational field or frequency, you can expect an expansion and elevation of consciousness. This energy is ideal to stimulate past-life memories and psychic activities.

Sedona has three electric vortexes (Bell Rock along with Courthouse Butte and Airport Mesa), one magnetic vortex (Cathedral Rock), and one electromagnetic vortex (Boynton Canyon Area).

Seminar participants have reported phenomenal experiences while meditating or using self-hypnosis in these environments. The experiences range from intense spiritual visions to impressions of what took place in these canyons long ago. Many have reported direct contact with spirit entities who remain here. One of the most common reports I've received is that automatic writing is more intensely successful here than anywhere else, and even those who are new to the technique usually have impressive results. Many of the participants have reported physical healings. For most newcomers, the entire area, not to mention the vortexes themselves, generates a physical change that virtually eliminates the need for sleep.

I have thousands of pages of reports of the experiences people have had in the vortexes. And yet, what is most convincing to me is the fact that I have personally experienced these things, as have those closest to me. As a great understatement, I can only say that my own psychic ability and spiritual experiences in the vortexes have never been surpassed anywhere else. They have included vivid visions, past-life recall, and physical healing.

Dick Sutphen, Sedona, Arizona, 1977

My very first encounter with one of the vortexes took place in the mid-1970s. A woman familiar with the area took me to Airport Mesa and then left, warning me not to venture into the vortex itself or even to dangle my feet over the edge. She claimed a friend of hers who had done that ended up with severe blisters on the bottoms of his feet. After sitting and meditating a while, I walked to the edge of the rise overlooking the vortex and held my hands out over it. I could actually feel a force or a pressure pushing against my palms.

With all my work and experience in metaphysics as a guide, I decided that the area held no danger and decided to ignore the woman's warning and climb down into the vortex. What followed was an amazing afternoon of meditation, past-life experiences, and a feeling of recharged aliveness.

There were no adverse physical or mental effects. In fact, as an interesting side note on this day, I was one day into a case of intestinal influenza that was hitting everyone in our area at the time. Most felt the effects for four days or more. Yet, on emerging from the vortex, all signs of the flu were gone and I experienced no more of it.

I decided the woman's friend was either a true "tenderfoot" and got the blisters from hiking to the vortex, or perhaps he was experiencing some negativity within himself or some karmic manifestation brought out by the vortex energy.

Since then, I have visited the vortexes numerous times with no ill effects. That is not to say that some people do not have negative or even dangerous experiences. I will discuss things to look out for when visiting the vortexes in Chapter 6: Vortex Locations and Warnings.

Most vortex experiences are transforming, spiritual, and totally renewing. The following are just a few of the thousands of reports I've received about extraordinary vortex experiences. In quoting these experiences here and throughout this book, I have included the individuals' initials and the city and state in which they live. However, some individuals preferred to remain anonymous, so their names have been withheld.

Perhaps their reasons are similar to those expressed by Sedona Psychic Seminar participant M.P. of Virginia Beach, Virginia, who lamented, "I have only two regrets: that the seminar is over, and that I must return home and can't tell anyone about my experiences—not even the men I date. The eastern portion of the United States is not 'enlightened.' Even those who have a tendency to 'believe' are extremely skeptical."

However, our research and the positive responses to our seminars and our products show there are in fact many "enlightened" individuals in the eastern United States. The problem seems to be that when a person has a unique and unusual psychic experience like those encountered by many in Sedona, they are often afraid to mention it to others for fear of being labeled "weird" or "crazy." Therefore, you may have among your friends and acquaintances many who have had similar experiences to your own but who were afraid to mention them to you.

Part of creating your own reality is drawing to yourself the types of people with whom you can interact on an honest and forthright basis. If your dates or friends think you're weird because you have experienced psychic phenomena, maybe you're dating or associating with the wrong people. By opening yourself up, you may be surprised with similar revelations from friends and lovers.

Obviously, "telling all" in your business environment or "pushing" your metaphysical ideas on unaccepting people is not in your best interest. But you often may find that by being yourself, your life and your relationships become better and better.

Thousands of my Sedona Psychic Seminar participants have described incredible metaphysical experiences here, ranging from direct contact with spirits to visions to healings. In the following pages, many of these experiences are told in their own words. In Chapters 4 and 5, we also hear from Gregory Frazier and Kathie Dame-Glerum, who share their vast knowledge of Sedona.

Another thing I should mention here is that the participants reporting these events are not all professional psychics or those who make their living in metaphysical pursuits. They are nurses, teachers, military personnel, homemakers, and business professionals of all types. They look and act just like your neighbors, friends, and relatives. Being psychic is not "weird" or unusual. Everyone is psychic to some degree. Those with an interest, like those who attend seminars or study metaphysical ideas on their own, are able to expand their abilities to see, feel, and experience more than what our "normal" five senses tell us.

Often, being in a place of increased energy, such as Sedona, expands that type of higher consciousness more rapidly. Many of the people who have written to me say they never considered themselves to be psychic and were often amazed at their own experiences there. Many had unusual experiences in Sedona before ever knowing it was a psychic energy vortex area.

But because the stigma still exists, for those who would rather not have us identify them, we respect their wishes and thank them and all those mentioned in this book for allowing us to publish the fantastic results of their experiences. In fact, you may see certain individuals' names more than once as many encountered several different types of experiences or wrote to us after each of several Sedona visits.

Whether identified or not, the accounts are presented in the individuals' own words. Many letters have been edited for clarity or space considerations, as some numbered 20 pages or more!

As bizarre and amazing as these incidents are, those who experienced them insist that they really happened.

"Holding a change pouch and a watch belonging to my deceased father, I tried to contact him in Boynton Canyon. The battery in the watch had been dead for many months, yet I hadn't replaced it. I had barely begun meditation when the watch began to work. I had not set it (and still haven't) but it has been keeping correct Arizona time since then."

M.P.
Virginia Beach, Virginia

(Note: This was written 24 days after her vortex visit.)

"I realized just how protected we were in the vortex. We were exploring a rather rugged area and I fell. I don't mean just losing my balance—I WAS FALLING! [My friend] made a grab for me but missed. I thought, *Oh, well, what better place to die*. I was stopped at that moment by a very solid but gentle force and pushed up on my feet.

"At first, I thought [my friend] had succeeded in grabbing me, but as I was being pushed up, I turned and looked at her. She was staring in total disbelief. . . . Since then, I've always felt very protected and peaceful in the vortex."

N.H.
Mesa, Arizona

"I knew nothing of psychic forces, vortexes, or the like when I first traveled to Sedona in 1973. I was a tourist, an avid shopper, and a weaver. I came down Oak Creek Canyon from Flagstaff—a thrilling drive of hairpin turns and sheer cliffs—and entered another world.

"Even then I felt drawn to the area. I was energized and cleansed in a way I didn't understand and I said later that Sedona had an atmosphere that couldn't be defined.

"When I returned home to New Hampshire, I wove a wall hanging of a large rock formation which I thought was representative of all the wonderful bluffs and cliffs I had seen.

"A few years later, I again traveled to Arizona, and quite naturally, to Sedona. While I was there, I photographed a large rock formation to which I felt especially attracted—one I had not seen on my previous trip. I later learned that this particular rock is called 'Bell Rock' because of its distinctive domed shape.

"When I again returned home and had my pictures developed, I was amazed to find that the photograph of Bell Rock matched the wall hanging I had woven almost three years before! Even the cloud formations were similar.

"This time, when I arrived in Sedona, I climbed part way up Bell Rock to meditate. I have never felt so peaceful. I was floating and couldn't feel my body at all.

"I saw . . . symbols, like hieroglyphics, but I couldn't tune into them. I asked what message I was to carry back to me from the energies of Bell Rock and it was simply this: 'We are here. We exist.'

"On a deeper level, I think the message is that we are all part of the same consciousness, the same life force. We can be in touch with other forms of consciousness if we listen for them and follow our own inner urges, which will guide us all on our own paths of awareness.

"Before going to Bell Rock, I had bought a crystal with blue highlights. When I finished meditating on Bell Rock, it had turned purple and is still purple to this day."

T.G.
Auburn, New Hampshire

(Note: Seminar participants often want to take home a small red rock, crystals, or other memento of the vortexes. All are asked to request permission from vortex spirits before removing anything—stones, twigs, etc., from these sacred areas. And, of course, removing desert plants or artifacts of any kind is forbidden by law.)

"I had several interesting experiences, including becoming so 'charged up' in the Airport Mesa that I was 'flying' for two days. I worked with a pendulum in all four vortexes and noticed these interesting results: In the positive vortexes (Airport Mesa and Bell Rock), the pendulum gave its usual responses, but in the negative vortexes (Cathedral [Rock] or Courthouse [Butte]), all responses were opposite in direction.

"For example, a positive response is normally, and in the positive vortexes, clockwise for me, and a negative response is back and forth from side to side. In the negative vortex, the positive response was counterclockwise and the negative response went back and forth, forward and backward. In Boynton Canyon, the balanced vortex, the pendulum seemed confused, and gave conflicting answers if asked the same question more than once. In all vortexes, the pendulum leaned away from the vortex from five to ten degrees.

"At Bell Rock, the pendulum guided me to some crystals, which I was given permission to take home."

P.A.S.
Derby, Kansas

"I was the woman at the seminar who came up to ask about why my palms got so hot after meditating and you told me, after asking many questions, that I was probably a natural healer. Soon after returning home, I cut myself rather badly with a large knife. My hands were still warm each time I remembered the self-hypnosis, so I concentrated on this and the cut healed without a scar. I told my husband, a minister, about it and he merely said that there are many things God has given us that we simply don't understand.

"I began to have severe sleep problems and it turned out that my thyroid had gone hyper (called Graves' disease). Of three possible treatments, they thought burning it out with a large dose of radiation would be best. I was burned from the inside out; had a lot of pain, and then began to have terrible headaches. I finally decided that if there were to be any healing within me, I would have to get it together and help myself. These headaches would wake me bolt upright and my throat would hurt so much that I wanted to tear it out of my neck. So I prayed that if it were true that God had given me the power to heal, that this power would be available to use on myself. My hands got very hot. I laid them over my throat where the pain was, and the pain stopped completely."

C.D.

"I was at the Airport [Mesa] Vortex. A ring I was wearing on my left hand began to vibrate, and I felt great energy in the hand. I was not in deep trance, just relaxed. I had my eyes open. I brought my watercolors with me and did a painting. It was the first time I had done anything creative in a long time. I was told to use my middle name to sign my painting. This has always been a question in the back of my mind as my first name is rather plain, but I felt that my middle name is too pretentious. It was an extremely emotional experience. I'm sure I will never be the same. I had the feeling it was telling me to be myself and not be so serious."

M.B.F.
Panguitch, Utah

"At Boynton Canyon, I meditated in hopes of having a psychic higher-consciousness experience with my late husband, who died two-and-a-half years ago. I believe that connection was made and we were able to have a final, inclusive, closing conversation. This was very satisfying to me as he had died instantly in a car accident. I found myself discussing all the significant moments of our marriage and how I have grown and developed in ways I wouldn't have imagined. All the anger I felt melted away finally.

"I believe that conversation enabled us to let our relationship go free this time around with love and understanding and a great deal of appreciation for each other. I will never forget Boynton Canyon."

M.H.
Portland, Oregon

"It's easier to be 'open' in an accepting, feeling environment. On Bell Rock, the capricious spirit whom I love, who had chosen to kill himself three years ago on this day, made sure I knew that he had really arrived. He jabbed me in the ribs and brought me to my feet—flat out of meditation. We know I don't convince casually! One reason I am here is to accept what I know—that I had to *not* stop him from doing what he did."

L.J.
Rockledge, Florida

CHAPTER 1

PSYCHIC MIGRATION

Upon first arriving in Sedona, you cannot help but perceive a subtle but powerful force. The vortex energy expands and intensifies your own energy and the energy generated between people. If the existing energy is primarily positive, it increases the positive quality. The reverse is also true: the vortex energy will intensify negativity, which can be undesirable.

Because of these intense vibrations, when couples move to Sedona, their relationship either becomes far better than it was previously, or the intensity pulls them apart and the relationship ends. I've always felt it's a subconscious karmic decision when a couple decides to relocate here. And many do so as a result of spontaneously arrived at decisions.

Here are more testimonials from seminar participants that demonstrate this phenomenon.

"I first came to Sedona to attend Dick's May 1984 Sedona Psychic Seminar. When not at the seminar, all I could do was cry and say, 'I am *home!*' I called home to Riverside, California, and told my husband, 'We are moving!' We arrived in Sedona to live in April 1985. Home *at last!*"

R.M.
Sedona, Arizona

"My husband and I were ready for a change. We were living in Princeton, New Jersey, and felt an urge to move West. I was researching the Anasazi and wanted to find a central location where I could do my work. We remembered driving through Sedona once very quickly on our way somewhere else and remembered we liked the town, but we couldn't remember anything about it. Can you imagine? We didn't 'remember' the red rocks or anything! But right then we decided to move there anyway and we've lived here happily now for three years."

K.D.G.
Sedona, Arizona

"As soon as we began driving down from the airport, I had the feeling of coming home. I seemed to know where everything was, although I have never been to Sedona before, plus a very calm, peaceful feeling, a feeling of finally belonging.

"At the Boynton Canyon Vortex, I did a short meditation and asked whether I should move to Arizona as I have been planning to do so for about two years. My answer, upon coming out of meditation, was a cloud in the shape of an arrowhead, pointing directly at the large monolith-like rock. I took this to be a very visually affirmative answer."

P.A.
Council Bluffs, Iowa

"I found upon leaving Sedona a feeling of leaving home. This was my first visit, but the place captured my heart and I know I will be returning to Sedona regularly."

Name Withheld
Long Beach, California

"In the year and a half I have lived in Sedona, it has come to me very strongly that no one is meant to live here permanently and that no one is to own this land. It belongs to all. It is a place of vision quest, a place whose vortex energies intensify and accelerate whatever you have brought with you. Are you ready to know your strengths and weaknesses? To know what role you are to perform in this play called life? To truly know yourself? If so, then Sedona is the place for you.

"I first came to Sedona in May of 1985 for a brief vacation. At one point, I had an experience during an afternoon meditation. In my vision, I was on a road under the red cliffs surrounding me. At first, the road curved gently, but my mind said, 'No, no, it must be straight.' It straightened out and I heard a voice say, 'This one goes all the way to Moscow.' Then, just as suddenly as I had left, I was back in a conscious state. I had no idea what had happened to me. Two weeks after returning home, I received an article from a friend concerning ley lines [which are lines of natural magnetic currents], I realized the significance of my experience.

"Sedona began to haunt me. I had a photo of the spot where I had my experience blown up and placed in my office.

"In December of 1987, my brother and I came to Sedona to pray for world peace at Bell Rock. It was like coming home. I had another vivid psychic experience in which I picked up on the near-death of an aunt that occurred that evening. By this time, I knew that I wanted to live in Sedona someday.

"I returned 'home' in June of 1988. My brother again came with me and we met our sister and brother-in-law in Sedona and went to the vortex areas. Even my born-again Christian sister felt the energies.

"Shortly after returning home, I went to a lecture and met some friends I hadn't seen for a while. They asked me what I was up to. I replied that I was moving to Sedona on July 15th. I had no idea I was going to say this, it just popped out. Once said, though, I followed through. I gave two weeks' notice at my workplace and came to Sedona on July 16th with no place to live, no job, and very little money. The next day, I had a place to live, and within nine days, I had a job. My family back in California, whom I love dearly, and my life there were like a distant dream. I had come to Sedona to know myself and the process was starting.

"My story is a common one here. Some consciously know why they have come here, others do not. Once we are here, our learning is made easy or difficult by our acceptance or non-acceptance of what we discover about ourselves.

"Although I have had a few down times, my own processing has been exciting and fulfilling because I have been open to it. However, I have seen others suffer much and have to leave. It is what we make of it.

"At present, I am feeling at peace and rather finished with the Sedona energies. They have worked their magic on me. It is time for me to leave Sedona and create a space for someone else who needs to be here. I will live on the periphery, going in and out as I am pulled and helping others in their processing as I am asked. I thank God for this beautiful place that is meant to be shared with all."

Y.K.
Sedona, AZ

"As soon as we entered Sedona, I spoke to the real estate agent about property values in Sedona. I promised to get back to him but I never got the opportunity to do so.

"My friends and I stayed over one more day after the Sedona Psychic Seminar so that we could explore the vortexes at our leisure. We went to Bell Rock and I climbed to a comfortable level and settled down to say my rosary. I have been troubled and uncertain for many months now. My husband is paralyzed on his right side from a stroke, and other personal factors in my life have left me feeling as though I am in limbo. Upon completing my prayers, I put my head down on my knees and prayed that I be shown the way, that I receive confirmation of things to come, that I was on the right path, and that I be given a sign.

"Suddenly, I began slowly rocking from side to side, the tears streamed uncontrollably down my face, and the rocking became stronger and stronger. As it increased in intensity, I became very frightened and called to my friends. They came and placed their hands on my shoulders and gradually the rocking stopped.

"After leaving the vortex, we made our way back to the real estate agent. He showed me a home in the Chapel development, directly below the Chapel of the Holy Cross and in clear view of Bell Rock, where I had received my inspiration. I gave him a down payment and purchased the home. I certainly had been given a sign. It was an experience I shall never forget. I know I was guided there."

**K.K.
Stanton, California**

Lots of people have been heeding the call to move West since the early '70s. I wrote about this phenomenon in my book *Past Lives, Future Loves*.

For many years, Arizona has been a leading psychic center in the country. The psychic concentration is within a 100-mile circle that includes Phoenix, Scottsdale, Sedona, and Prescott. The Phoenix/Scottsdale metropolitan area, of course, is well known. Prescott is a typical old Arizona cowboy town situated in a mountain valley and surrounded by a national forest preserve. Like Sedona, it is rapidly becoming a haven for those wishing to escape the stress of big-city life.

People from everywhere have been, and are being, directed to relocate to the Prescott/Sedona area, and they have moved their entire families thousands of miles because they felt it was important. Also, psychic practitioners, writers, and those dedicated to philosophy come in increasing numbers.

Whenever I ask newcomers why, the answer is always, "We were told to come." There are many psychic migration theories and none of them negates the others, so all could be valid. Most have to do with "energy." In the Bradshaw Mountain area, some say it is the mountaintop elevation and the pine trees. Pine trees are supposed to provide more live energy to the atmosphere than any other plant or tree. It is a somewhat generally accepted belief that if you stand on the north side of a pine tree and hug it, you will be "recharged."

I don't know if I accept that or not, but it's an interesting idea and I've been known to hug a few myself.

In Los Angeles, an old Sioux Indian woman—a shaman who had once worked with Black Elk—told me, "I've had a great vision and in it Chief Gall came to me and told me to go to Arizona. It was here that the movement would form and spread. A symbol would guide the way."

Many feel that something is supposed to happen here or from here. Sedona is supposedly situated over an ancient Lemurian city and many have experienced impressions of confirmation of this concept, which I'll talk more about in Chapter 3 (see page 25).

There is something about the energy source of the entire area that no one really understands. Phoenix has always been known as "the valley of healing," even by the original American Indians who settled there. A "special" energy is again given as the reason. There are hundreds of metaphysically oriented churches and organizations in the Phoenix metropolitan area.

Another concept is that all great religions or spiritual philosophies have been launched from desert areas. Supposedly, desert energy is conducive to evolutionary thinking. Prescott and Sedona are surrounded by high desert, and Phoenix and Scottsdale are in the Sonoran Desert.

Maybe it is "energy" that is pulling people together. Past-life soul group energy, some cosmic energy as in the Sedona vortexes, or the mental energies of like-minded people. It doesn't matter how, only that there is evident momentum.

If these things are happening by "plan," then I feel it is your plan and only through your own acceptance will changes occur. You will certainly never be forced to develop psychic abilities or find out about your past lives and associations or to relocate to a metaphysical geographic location.

You control and create your own reality in these things as in all others.

Of all the areas of the southwest, Arizona seems to be the most mystical, the most spiritual, and contains some of the most beautiful areas known anywhere in the world. Even the origin of the name *Arizona* is a mystery. Cynics might tell you it stands for "arid zone."

However, in 1877, journalist Hiram C. Hodge published a book about his travels in Arizona from 1874 to 1876. In his book, reprinted in 1965 under the title *Arizona As It Was, 1877*, Hodge related what he claims was an Aztec legend that explains the origin of the name:

Of the origin and significance of the name Arizona, there seems to be much doubt, and a score or more of definitions have been given by different and well-informed persons. Referring back to the old Aztec traditions, the following significant item occurs, which may assist somewhat in the explanation:

"The earth is the offspring of the sky. Long prior to the present race of men, the earth was peopled by a race of giants who in time died off, leaving the earth uninhabited. After a long time, a celestial virgin, a child of one of the thirteen deities who rule all things, came down to the earth, and being well pleased, remained for a long time its sole inhabitant. Once when in a deep sleep, a drop of dew from heaven fell on her, and she conceived and bore two children, a son and daughter, from whom have sprung all the people of the earth. The name of this celestial virgin was Arizunna, "the beautiful, or sun beloved maiden." The Mohave language, which is by far the most perfect and complete of any of the . . . dialects of the country, has two words of nearly the same meaning: *Ari*, meaning the sun, holy, good, or beautiful; and *Urnia*, maid or maiden; which together means the land of the beautiful or lovely maiden. This may be the true meaning of the word *Arizona*. Another definition is this, *Ari*, from the Mohave, meaning beautiful or good, and *Zona*, from the Spanish, a zone, and taken together, meaning the land of the beautiful zone. Both of these definitions are well made, and are quite significant and expressive.[1]

It is a well-established fact that in the time when Hodge was writing about Arizona, the white man was abysmally ignorant of the American Indian tribes of the area. Therefore, we cannot be sure this legend is indeed from the Aztec. Referring to his mention of perfection of the Mohave language, it is interesting to note that the Mohave are one of many tribes that speak a language that is related to the language of the Yavapai. These languages are known as Yuman languages. Also, the Yavapai were often mistakenly called Mohave-Apache. In fact, the government agency in charge of setting up the reservation originally named it the Fort McDowell Mohave-Apache Community of the Fort McDowell Indian Reservation, even though they are Yavapai. It is now the Fort McDowell Yavapai Nation.

The Mohave referred to the Yavapai as the "people of the sun" (*enyaeva* meaning sun; *pai* meaning the people). This information becomes increasingly interesting when compared to the American Indian legends surrounding Sedona, which we will explore in the next chapter.

CHAPTER 2

SEDONA'S HISTORY AND LEGENDS

Sedona is located 120 miles north of Phoenix in the central Arizona mountains at a 4,300-foot elevation. The area is known as "red-rock country" because the magnificent red-rock formations are unique in the state and cover only a few square miles. Sedona's beautiful terrain is often featured in national publications and as the background in many television commercials. More than 75 major motion pictures have been filmed there, especially big-budget epic Westerns.

Modern Sedona is an art colony with outstanding galleries and is the home of many well-known artists and writers. The village of Tlaquepaque has become world-famous as an architectural showpiece of Spanish Colonial design. It houses major galleries and shops and is a highlight to the millions of annual visitors.

Sedona was founded June 26, 1902, when the post office was established. According to Albert E. Thompson in "The Story of Sedona" from the book *Those Early Days. Oldtimers' Memoirs*—a collection of old-timers' memoirs published by the Sedona Westerners—before 1902 the place was known as Camp Garden. It was named Sedona after the United States Post Office Department rejected the name Schnebly Station as being too long for postmarks. Sedona Schnebly and her husband, Theodore C. Schnebly, had settled there a year before. Schnebly became the first postmaster.

But where did Sedona Schnebly get her unusual name? According to her son, Ellsworth M. Schnebly, who wrote "How Sedona Was Named" in *Those Early Days. Oldtimers' Memoirs,* it was a product of Sedona's mother's inspiration:

> Numerous uninformed, and perhaps, well-intentioned people have speculated on how Sedona got its name and what the name means. Sedona is not an [American] Indian nor a Mexican name. One omnipotent individual explained it this way: When T. C. was courting Sedona, he said, "This weekend I am going over to see Dona." (Note: According to this same account, Sedona became known affectionately by her neighbors as "Aunt Dona.")
>
> My mother's parents were Pennsylvania Dutch and did not even know any Mexicans or [American] Indians back there . . . they reared twelve children including my mother. Grandmother said that she did not know why, but that she liked Sedona as a name and gave it to my mother. She had never heard of the name and after all, there is a first time that any word or name is used.

The American Indians hold the Sedona red-rock area as sacred. Legends passed down through generations tell of a goddess with supernatural powers who lived there and passed the ancient knowledge to the Yavapais through her grandson, The First Man.

Before she died in 1966 at the age of 88, Yavapai Chief Viola Jimulla related her remembrance of the legend to

Franklin Barnett, who published it in his biography of her, *Viola Jimulla: The Indian Chieftess*:

> The legend about the creation of the Yavapai . . . is based upon the belief that there were, or are, four different cycles or worlds. The first people emerged from underground and were terminated by the flood; the second was the time of the Goddess Komwida Pokwee (Old Woman Rock) and her grandson Skata-amcha (Skadkama); the third ended by world fire; and we are living in the fourth today. The story is that they, the Yavapais, came from underground and that they climbed through a large hole made by a huge pine tree with vines hanging from the tree into the hole. They used the vine to pull themselves to the surface of the earth.
>
> Komwida Pokwee, as a girl, came from the flood (first cycle of Yavapai creation) and settled in the Red Rock country near what is now Sedona. She came when the earth was still wet (second cycle of creation). Komwida Pokwee is the Goddess of the supernatural and medicine powers, and is beautiful and as pure as a downy white feather. Skata-amcha is her grandson and all of the songs, supernatural powers, and medicine power and knowledge were given to him by his grandmother, and were passed on to the Yavapai medicine men and their people. The medicine men, or anyone believing in the religion, may see her yet in a vision or dream and receive instructions, comfort, and encouragement. These two, together, Komwida Pokwee and Skata-amcha, always set a good example for our Yavapai people to follow.[1]

Unfortunately, like the Yavapai people themselves, these legends have become scattered and lost.

Comparison of Viola's version to that of Mike Harrison, born in 1886, oldest man of the Fort McDowell Yavapai community, and John Williams, born 1904, shows similar concepts but different details.

This account was taken from the book *The Yavapai of Fort McDowell* by Sigrid Khera:

We come out at Sedona, the middle of the world. This is our home. . . . We call Sedona *Wipuk*. We call it after the rocks in the mountains there. Some of my people, they call themselves *Wipukpa*. That's the ones who live up there around Sedona. All Yavapai come from Sedona. But in time they spread out.

North of Camp Verde there is Montezuma Well. We call it *Ahagaskiaywa*. The lake has no bottom and underneath the water spread out wide. That's where the people come out first. . . .

That first chief from down the Well, we see him on the sky early in the morning. He is up there, the morning star. Lots of people come up from there, quail, rabbits, jackrabbits. And at the time when they are up, they all speak Yavapai. They get up on top and when they look back the water is coming. . . . The flood is in the Well. But the water doesn't come out. Just stays level in there. . . .

After some time there comes another flood. The people put a girl in a hollow log. Put food in that log for her. The woodpecker made a small hole for her in the log. Then they tell her: "The flood will raise you. You will hit the sky. But just lay still. If you lay still, you will get out in the end." Then the people glued the log together with pitch.

The girl lay still in there all the time. After some time, the water went down. The girl had a dove with her and she sent that dove out. She sent her out and the dove come back with a little seed. So the water was gone. There at Sedona there is a high place. It is the highest place all around. And when the water went down, the log hit that high place. It stopped right there. And the girl came out from the log.

We call that girl *Kamalapukwia*. That means "Old Lady White Stone." She had a white stone. And that white stone is the one which protects the women. Her name means she got that kind of stone. She is the first woman on earth and she got that stone. She is the first woman and we come from her. She came out at Sedona and that's where all [American] Indians come from.

Kamalapukwia lived in a cave in Sedona. Kamalapukwia was all alone. One morning she ran over to Mingus Mountain. Lay down there before the sun came up. The sun comes up and hits her inside. After that she went to that Cave where the water drips down all the time. She lay down and the water came down and hit her. Made her a baby. A little girl.

When that girl came to age, Kamalapukwia said to her, "Daughter, they did that and you come up. You go over there and do like I did. So we have another people." They were the only two people. So they were lonely and wanted another human. The girl said, "All right." . . . She got pregnant and then got the little baby, it was a boy: Sakarakaamche.

When that boy was still a baby, a bald eagle killed his mother. . . . Now there were only two people: the old lady Kamalapukwia and the little boy Sakarakaamche. The old lady raised the little boy. . . .

15

The old lady, she told Sakarakaamche everything. Taught him everything. And he learned from his father, the Cloud. Sakarakaamche knew everything about the weeds which cure all sicknesses (from his grandmother). We don't know where she learned it, but Sakarakaamche learned it from her. And he is the one who is teaching the humans who come up. . . .

He gave us four sacred things: he gave us the Blackroot, the yellow powder, the blue stone, and the white stone.

Blackroot is a very great medicine. We call it *isamaganyach*. It helps against pains and sores. It makes you feel good again.

The yellow powder, we call it *achitawsa*. It is the pollen from the cattail. The medicine man, when he heals somebody, he puts yellow powder on him. Yellow powder stands for the light. It helps you think and talk right.

The blue stone and white stone, that's what protects us from bad things. The blue stone stands for men, the white stone for the women. When you have these stones and think well, bad things can't hit you. The blue stone that people wear on a ring, that's not the one that protects them. It is like a toy. But when it is blessed by a medicine man, then it will help.[2]

We can't be certain, but from the story of the Yavapai men, we would assume that the blue stone and the white stone they are referring to are turquoise, so prominent in jewelry of all Southwestern American Indian tribes, and white quartz crystal, which is found embedded in the red rocks of Sedona.

One thing that has always interested me is the number of people who, after experiencing the vortexes at Sedona, relate having experiences with spirits. These experiences seem to correlate with these very obscure American Indian legends, of which I have not previously written or talked about to seminar participants. The extent of our knowledge before researching this book was the story we had heard that Boynton Canyon near Sedona was home of the Great Mother.

These legends are not widely known, even in local areas, as little is written about the Yavapai. Because white soldiers moved the Yavapai to many different areas in Arizona in the late 1800s, they were often mistaken for members of other tribes. They were even thought to be a branch of the Apache tribe, to which they are not at all related, even by language. We have had to do quite a bit of searching in local Arizona libraries to find these somewhat rare books about the Yavapai.

Even though we are, for the first time, publishing the accounts of these legends, it is amazing that experiences of participants of past Sedona Psychic Seminars relate specific details that correspond to these ancient tales.

For instance, many claim to see spirits or guides, a not too unlikely situation since, being in the West, one might relate his or her experiences to Western concepts of "cowboys and Indians." However, rarely does anyone ever claim to see pioneers, covered wagons, cowboys, or gold miners, all of which were also very prevalent in the area.

In fact, I have had only two reports regarding such experiences in Sedona seminars. One man saw himself as a cowboy in a past life who was rejected by his contemporaries because he defended the plight of the indigenous people. He eventually went to live with his American Indian brothers. A woman who experienced being a pioneer woman in a past life gave this account: "While in meditation, listening to the joyous laughter of the children on your 'sounds' tape and viewing a scene of me in an early settler's home on the prairie, for some unexplained reason, the laughter made me, a pioneer woman, want to cry. What had happened back then?"

Many possibilities, either from a present life situation or a past life, may have triggered this woman's tears. It is known that empathetic individuals often are able to pick up the vibrations of past events in an area. With this in mind, it is interesting to note that the pioneer woman for whom Sedona was named suffered a tragedy with one of her children. Because of it, she had to leave the area and spent several years in emotional recovery before returning to Sedona.

Because of the sacredness of this area to the American Indians, it seems that most of the vibrations picked up by those in Sedona have to do with them. Another statement from the two Yavapai men might explain why this is, and why it may not be just participants' imaginations. The American Indians believe that spirits inhabit the sacred places, especially the mountainous areas. They even claim that under certain conditions, these spirits are visible:

> The Kakaka are just like [American] Indians, but little people. Maybe three or four feet high. They live in the mountains, Four Peaks, Red Mountain, Superstition [Mountains], Granite Mountain near Prescott. They can get in and out the mountain. They are just like the wind, like air. You can hear them hollering at night and sometimes some people can see them. The Kakaka never die. They were around this country before the people. . . . They keep watching over us all the time.

Others experience the visitation of an American Indian woman or women, and I suppose, because we have talked about the concept of the Great Mother, some may relate what they see to that idea. But there are a greater than average number of visions and experiences that relate directly to the story of the Goddess and her daughter. Even the details of many individuals' experiences seem similar. Also, it's worth noting how birds play a role in the perceptions. Remember that the Goddess sent a dove out of the log—an eagle at the mother of The First Man. The color white is also prevalent. Chief Viola described the Goddess as "beautiful and pure as a downy white feather."

The following are just some of the experiences related by seminar participants that feature the indigenous peoples of Sedona.

"At Airport Mesa, I had a strong feeling of peace and perceived a gentle female presence. Then I saw the Great Mother weep. She is a very tall, slender woman who wears a white dress. The crows play in her hair. The sparrow and the eagle became symbols of the Great Mother."

P.C.
Pacifica, California

"We visited Boynton Canyon and found a spot in the dry creek bed where we laid our crystals out to charge in the sun. Right before we decided to leave, I felt a shaking of my soul as I perceived a huge [American] Indian woman rise from the center of the canyon. She stood about 200 feet tall and was dressed in white buckskin. She was beautiful. I sat there in awe. She looked at me and smiled, then turned slowly, motioning to all of the area as if to say, 'This is my land. I am guardian here.' She was slowly enveloped by the canyon floor once again. It wasn't until we returned to the seminar that Dick explained about the Great Mother. I know I saw her."

R.M.
Sedona, Arizona

"Cathedral Rock: A smiling young woman dressed in white—apparently *mestizo* (Spanish/[American] Indian mix). 'The serious search for spiritual development must be balanced with joy and happiness—and will be.' Her name: Neena."

F.H.S.
Gaithersburg, Maryland

"At Cathedral or Courthouse Rock, one of the resident birds swooped at me and yelled just as I was calling the vortex spirit. As we were leaving, I was given a feather from the wing tip of an eagle. This has a special significance since the name of the vortex spirit who worked with me and [with] whom I have a past-life tie is Eagle Feather. Also, in that past life, I was a leader and medicine man of the Eagle Clan."

P.A.S.
Derby, Kansas

"I did have a very brief flash of two images. One was that of an . . . eagle god. He was suspended with arms spread out, in front of the cliffs across the valley, and had eagle feathers on his arms and body. The second image was right behind the eagle god and was of cliff dwellings."

R.H.W.
Woodland Hills, California

"With my eyes open, I studied the face of the rock formations, seeing the faces of [American] Indians and animals."

E.K.H.
Birmingham, Michigan

"In Boynton Canyon, I became very aware of [the American] Indian presence. It was peaceful and loving, but I also sensed it was their ground. We were to absorb and learn from the vibrations offered for the advancement of humankind."

S.T.
Lawndale, California

As Yavapai Chief Viola Jimulla stated, " . . . anyone believing in the religion, may see her [the Goddess] yet in a vision or dream and receive instructions, comfort, and encouragement."

Recall that the Yavapai men said, "That first chief from down the Well, we see him on the sky early in the morning. He is up there, the morning star."

Although Viola seems to be referring to a female guide, these details correspond to what another seminar participant wrote about receiving instructions.

"We hiked into Boynton Canyon. After going into trance, I did some automatic writing. Here is what I wrote: 1058, a village of Pueblo Indians lived here in the area 2,500 years. There was a great flood in the canyon, many people died. I was saved. Morning Star is my name. You saw me dancing in your dream last night. I am one of your guides.

"My one son became Chief Towatchapee when his father died. My son died young in a battle with other [American] Indians; there was much grief and wailing. My father was the tribal medicine man. After the flood, we moved to the village where Sedona is now. I lived to be 60 years old."

A.J.J.
Pleasanton, California

"After the vortex orientation, my companions and I headed for Boynton Canyon. From what we had heard and read, this seemed to be the place for us. When we were about two miles from the vortex, someone remarked that they were feeling very calm and peaceful. The words that suddenly came out of my mouth were: 'I don't. I feel like laughing.' And that is exactly what I did! I laughed, and the laughter grew until my sides hurt and tears were streaming down my face. I had difficulty catching my breath enough to stop. I felt as if I had been laughing a very long time, although the incident only lasted a few seconds. When the laughter stopped, the ache in my side went away.

"The laugh was not my laugh . . . it sounded like a young woman. Since I am not known for uncontrollable emotions, including laughter—my own being far more raucous when it can be heard, with the sound frequently catching in my throat—I knew that this was not my laughter. This was totally different: joyous, uninhibited, youthful, playful, almost tingling.

"As we were hiking out, talking, and sharing vortex experiences after having spent several hours in the vortex, the uncontrollable laughter began again. I tried to pay attention to the sound and how I felt, but I was over-come with the joyful laughter. I shared the information at the evening session and afterward was told by two women, who are doing research on the area, that they'd had a similar experience. They said their giggles had lasted for most of a weekend. They told me that, so far, they had only discovered one female spirit in the area; her name is Running Deer.

"Before the seminar, I dreamed about [American] In-dians, which is odd because I couldn't recall dream-ing about [them] before. The woman in the dream was [also] named 'Running Deer.'"

D.S.

"It took some time for me to relax and go into a med-itation. Then my guide came and took me to join [the American] Indians and I danced with them in their 'Friendship Dance.'

"I was given permission to take three small stones: one for my husband, one for me to use at home, and a tiny one to carry with me. I know the spirits are in the stones. When I hold them in my hand, I feel so calm, warm, and loving."

P.C.

CHAPTER 3

THE SEDONA/ LEMURIA CONNECTION

Another interesting correlation I have found in the experiences of seminar participants is that an ancient city existed in the area that is now Sedona. Many people have related visions of energy fields generated by crystals, advanced civilizations, or extraterrestrial beings, and some kind of cataclysmic event—most often a terrible flood. We have read in preceding chapters how the [American] Indian legends describe great floods and godlike beings who escaped the destruction. Does it all relate?

Since I first began spending time in Sedona, I've had metaphysically oriented people tell me [that] there is an ancient Lemurian city buried beneath the great red-rock formations and canyons that now comprise the terrain or that Sedona somehow relates to Lemuria. Close friends, whom I respect for their psychic abilities, have related visions of unusual, ancient structures that appear in various areas. Some have seen visions of these structures in the sky above Sedona.

In re-examining regressions [that] I have conducted with individuals over the years and comparing them with the trance communications of Edgar Cayce, Ruth Montgomery, and Lemuria's primary historian, Colonel James Churchward, I find general agreement about many facts regarding Lemurian history.

According to Churchward, Lemuria was a huge Pacific continent unconnected to what is now the North American continent. He relates four great cataclysms: the third, and worst, transpired 80,000 years ago. The final cataclysm took place 12,000 years ago, and sent "Mu" and millions of her inhabitants to the depths of the sea in a "vortex of fire and water."

This seems to relate quite closely with the Edgar Cayce trance readings. Both agree that the Lemurians had ample warning of the impending catastrophe; for centuries, people left the motherland to establish colonies in areas such as Egypt, Peru, Central America, and Mexico.

All the metaphysical writers and researchers seem to agree that the Lemurians were a spiritual, peaceful people. They developed a very just and fair governmental system; one of their great rulers was a woman. The populace was composed of highly skilled artisans and craftsmen. They enjoyed a very advanced form of civilization, with great cities and impressive temples, and many Lemurians attained a universal perspective.

There is speculation that a great land mass once existed above water in the Pacific where only Lemurian mountaintops remain today as islands. In the Mexican temple of Uxmal, an inscription declares that the structure was dedicated to the memory of Mu, "the lands to the west, that land of Kui, the birthplace of our sacred mysteries." The temple faces west, the direction of the lost Lemurian continent.

In her book *The World Before*, Ruth Montgomery, through automatic writing controlled by her guides, relates that the huge heads on Easter Island in the Pacific mark the site of a great Lemurian ceremonial center.

In Edgar Cayce's reading #812-1, the "sleeping prophet" talked about a woman named 'Amelelia,' a priestess in the Temple of Light, who was an overseer of communications between various lands. The reading mentions Mu and a "particular portion of Arizona and Nevada that are as a portion of the Brotherhood of those people from Mu."

According to Churchward, Lemuria was known as the "Land of the Sun" and "Empire of the Sun." In his book *The Sacred Symbols of Mu*, Churchward also claims that the cliff-dwelling American Indians of Arizona and New Mexico were once residents of Lemuria. The cliff dwellings of Montezuma's Castle are now maintained for public visitation by the U.S. Park Service, only a few miles from Sedona.

The Hopi reservation and mesas are also very close to Sedona. Hopi legend claims that the tribe came to their current area from the West after their world was destroyed. They traveled on bamboo rafts until coming to a wall of steep mountains that they climbed; as they looked back, they could see islands sinking behind them.

Another interesting fact, that may or may not relate to Lemuria, was pointed out to me by author and scientist Dr. Patrick Flanagan. Pat was studying United States air pollution maps attained via satellite. Only two places in this country indicated perfectly clear air: a tiny spot around the top of Mount Shasta in California and the area around Sedona, Arizona.

Sedona is higher than Phoenix and lower than nearby Prescott, so why should this be? Possible explanations could be in the intense energy emitting from the vortexes in Sedona, or as the Hopi believe, the area is a sacred, spiritual ground and is thus protected. And maybe, as several of my seminar participants perceived, there is a great Lemurian crystal buried beneath Sedona that is emitting the intense energy.

During the May 1984 Sedona Psychic Seminar, which I conducted with [the late] psychic Alan Vaughan, I decided to run an experiment. After little prior discussion, I hypnotized the participants and asked them to perceive any information they could attain regarding the Sedona/Lemuria connection. I left it open as to how they would attain the knowledge: ESP, remote viewing, general regressions, or simply tapping into the collective unconscious.

When the session was complete, we discussed the results as a group and attained a general consensus about the connection. I asked those who were willing to share their experiences to write them down. A distillation of their individual communications reveals that 23 people received the "essence" of ancient, highly evolved people who relate to Lemuria. Seven sensed that a large crystal lies buried somewhere beneath the red earth of the area. Some, interestingly, felt that the name Lemuria was incorrect.

Here, in their own words, are the experiences of some of the participants.

"People of Mu colonized the Sedona area after the great disaster of the motherland. Their original colony was leveled by a glacier which carved the canyons and is now beneath the earth. A large geometric-shaped crystal is beneath this area. This crystal is the real source of the vortex power."

T.K.H.
Glendale, California

"There is an ancient city beneath Sedona, but Lemuria does not sound right to me. There is a crystal temple here, as in Atlantis, hence the energy vortex. It is my feeling that souls are congregating together in places like Sedona. It's like a reward for a 'good incarnation'— after a few lives, the reward is getting to come back to your source. Sounds far-fetched, right? But there is a definite purpose and plan for this. Sedona is a place of departure and arrival; it feels like an airport terminal. The energy is of such a high vibration that it attracts those traveling on different places and dimensions as well as those already here. So here are different dimensional souls now merging with the souls that have been here a long time. Each is exploring and learning from the others. It is very exciting, intellectual, learning, and sharing. Like a conference of all the Nobel Prize winners."

S.L.P.
Pueblo, Colorado

"The name Lemuria is incorrect. I think it might be a 'chanted' sound, something like 'LaMu.' I visualized a giant monolith expressing tremendous energy. It is time to establish the latent powers within; that is why we have returned to our former home for reunion and recreation."

V.H.
Long Beach, New York

"A large crystal is buried beneath Sedona. Where Sedona is now, there was a city before. The name was not Lemuria; it was destroyed by another power, but not completely. The city still exists, but on a different frequency."

M.B.
Renton, Washington

"There is a crystal in Boynton Canyon where the land folds into itself; solstices, equinoxes, and planetary alignments give energy to the other vortexes. There is great rejuvenation here as there has always been.

"I perceived a Temple of Learning or Temple of Healing. I don't get a sense of any buildings at all. The life-forms of high light and high vibration didn't seem to need any. The Tenders of the Crystal, who were lower in vibration and lesser evolved, needed the shelter, however, and lived in the caves surrounding the area. The highly evolved forms transmitted knowledge wordlessly, through the use of the crystal.

"The Tenders of the Caves were not people to emulate. Knowledge of them will not serve any purpose; they were animalistic, keepers only, and not of the Knowledge. When the crystal was destroyed (covered?) during the earth changes, many of the Knowledgeable Ones chose simply to leave their bodies so that they could return to teach when the crystal was again found. And it was the ignorance of the Unknowledgeable Ones that kept the crystal hidden after the earth changes—hidden from those who would destroy it as well as those who would harness the power.

"In an altered state, I can picture the crystal quite clearly as a large, disc-shaped convex. It is now lying upside down.

"P.S.: I have a sense that great power could be had by charging a large crystal, placed in a circle of stone—each one gathered from the other vortex areas and laid in the sun—above the main crystal in Boynton Canyon."

K.D.G.
Sedona, Arizona

"I didn't have any experiences at the vortex on my first trip Saturday afternoon, but I sure could feel the power. Saturday night, in the regression, was a different story.

"I perceived that I was working on the support structure for a crystal. I knew that this was to throw a beam of energy, something like a laser beam. I headed a group that was devising a crystal to expand the power of the 'great crystal' to the farthest reaches of the earth. And I knew that there were people who worked at the 'great crystal' who were not happy with me for doing this because they were going to lose some control.

"When I responded to your next suggestion, Dick, I saw myself in a balloon basket—that doesn't seem to make sense, but I was looking down into a valley, and it seemed to be in this area, in the Sedona area. And there were two high gate posts with a gate going through it; beyond that, a huge concrete slab, or something flat, like a landing area. And to the right were the buildings where we were working on the crystal.

"I know that was here because the vortex was here. I also know that we were meeting with highly evolved beings who were giving us the plans on how to build this 'sending station.'

"My next impression was of a great explosion, and I knew the great crystal had been destroyed. I think some people attempted to manipulate the energy in an attempt to destroy us, but it must have backfired or something. I don't understand it; the experience has left me very shaken."

Name Withheld
Phoenix, Arizona

"I perceived a large buried crystal, or maybe a special stone, generating powerful energy, like a buried transmitter, in the Boynton Canyon area. My most intense impressions were of the great sense of love and harmony in this area."

C.R.
Fremont, California

"In the Lemurian regression, I was an old man with long, white hair and beard, shiny metallic dress and shoes. And I was in what appeared to be a cavelike room ablaze with light. The light came from crystals arranged in a pentagram. People would come to me, down escalator-like stairs, to be healed—or rather, to stay well. They would sit in the pentagram; it was as if everyone came to do this. It was just a part of the lifestyle and was necessary in order to stay well.

"The Sedona area was a healing center, and the healing was always conducted in the cave, which was definitely below the ground, deep in the earth. I was really impressed by the brightness of the crystals in the cave."

M.C.
Del Mar, California

"My guide took me to a cave that he said was the entrance to the inner city. It is in Boynton Canyon. The cave was dark, but crystals lit the way. The deeper we went into the cave, the [brighter] it became. We came around a curve, and the crystals were so brilliant that I thought [they] should hurt my eyes, but [they] didn't. There was a man waiting for us, and he showed us around. This was a great center for healing."

H.F.
Alhambra, California

"First of all, this was the clearest clairvoyant experience I have had since I first became interested in psychic abilities. It was the type of clear-seeing that I had always dreamed of and programmed for. I saw a type of stone arched bridge with large columns on each side. I wondered what that was, and then the stone bridge turned into a modern bridge, like in San Francisco, and then back into the ancient bridge. On the bridge were several men in long white robes walking in line. I wondered who they were and a voice told me that they were high priests from Lemuria crossing over (to the area now known as Sedona) to pray and raise their consciousness. And, in turn, Sedona's consciousness (energy) would be raised by their presence. Next, I saw the priests sitting in an area praying within a special design imprinted in the red earth. In asking about the source of the energy, I perceived large crystals beneath or inside the rock formations."

J.S.
Chicago, Illinois

Not one to have my curiosity satisfied easily, I decided to conduct the same experiment at each successive Sedona Psychic Seminar to see whether the experiences related by those in different groups would parallel those of the initial experiment. The results were utterly amazing! Not only did participants in each group describe the same kinds of experiences, but the events and images they perceived were nearly the same as the groups who attended other seminars. Each seminar group consisted of more than 150 people, so we now had the results of several hundred participants, all describing more or less the same types of images and situations. What caused all these people to perceive the same things?

As you read through the following reports, notice how they compare to the reports from the first experiment. Also notice how certain elements—crystals, unusual energy sources, floods, healing—seem to come up again and again. Not only are these themes repeated, but some participants even describe similar details, such as crystals aligned in certain patterns or underground waterways and rivers.

"I was shown that the Sedona area was a 'staging area' for the voluntary evacuation of the people of Lemuria after the catastrophe that destroyed their homeland on earth. I was shown a large round flat spaceship (some might call it a flying saucer) hovering over a flat-topped mesa, and being loaded with supplies for a long journey. I received the message, 'We came from space, and we are going home.'

"The Lemurians were given a choice to go or to stay here. Some chose to stay here; they eventually became the Hopi tribe. The crystals served as navigational aids as well as a power source for the airship. Many of them (crystals) were inside the mesa over which the airship hovered, and many others were scattered around in a planned pattern."

P.A.S.
Derby, Kansas

"I saw two beams of light shooting out of the universe in a cross formation into the Sedona area. I felt entities of nonphysical form arrive via these light beams. The energies adopted a physical form on the earth plane. Their purpose was to teach a small group of humans living in the area. They failed in that they overstepped the boundaries of their mission and instead dominated the Sedona natives. The beings who came to Sedona had a certain aggressiveness to their personalities and yet I saw no overt acts of aggression. It was more that the natives, being a passive culture, more or less allowed the newly arrived entities to take command."

M.L.A.
Clearwater, Florida

"My first impressions were of drowning, of huge waves cascading over the red rocks with a thunderous noise. However, I quickly rose above this to an overview where I immediately noticed a sky full of rainbows arching from one mesa to another all around me. *How beautiful*, I thought. A voice answered, 'Yes, but ships do not fly on rainbows. Look, they have had to force land all over in valleys flooded with water. The energy flow has been disrupted.' And suddenly I could see the wreckage, the turmoil, the destruction.

"The cave dwellers climbed out of the rocks and called themselves 'blessed.' The cave dwellers did not have a high spiritual or mental nature. I have been warned repeatedly not to search them out, that there was nothing in their contribution to this culture to emulate. They were simply 'what was left after the good souls departed.'"

K.D.G.
Sedona, Arizona

"I had been away from the Sedona area, perhaps off the earth, since the flooding surprised me. As I saw the canyon flooded about halfway to the top, I was convulsed with anguish for the lives that had been lost."

A.B.E.

"A Lemurian 'city' was here. It felt more like an information center. A large power pyramid made of energy was visible and rainbow-colored in the air over the Airport [Mesa] Vortex area. A wall, several hundred feet high and made of a smooth gray material, ran for miles on the east and north sides of the Sedona area. There were two runways that ran from a common point to the west. They seemed miles long. In the central part of the city was a large wooded park with herds of animals.

"Under Bell Rock is a large crystal that sits upright. It is about or slightly below ground level, or where the base flares into the surrounding area. There is also a group of crystals buried under this whole area. They are in a distinct pattern but the crystals are pointing in random directions. This pattern covers hundreds of acres in each direction. Under the area—I've lost the location—is a metal container, like a time capsule, with information from then to now, from them to us. When I asked again about the connection, it still said a passing on or continuation of information."

R.S.

"The first image I got was of a lake with [American] Indians in canoes [as well as] a feeling of rather extensive submerged waterways used for communication/transportation of some kind. I also got an image/feeling of a huge time machine used for time travel or astronomical research. This was underground. In another underground area was one or more rooms used for magic."

R.H.W.
Woodland Hills, California

"This was more ancient than Lemuria, which was situated nearer the Pacific Ocean. This is the most ancient place for entities from other planets to come to this earth. They are still coming. This energy is from time immemorial. You are here for you have all been a part of the growth of this planet, from this area as well as other places on the earth. Those who can stand in the light will remain, the others will become nothing. Acknowledge your inheritance and give thanks."

D.K.
Aptos, California

"The Inner Temple was like a crystal cave. When the high priests were to enter a state of exteriorization [sic] the higher realms they would visit would give them more insight and knowledge on how to handle the problems they encountered in the earth's dimension. The crystal cave seemed to impart a knowledge and healing effect. When the high priests would leave their earth bodies, they became . . . light. The sounds inside the cave were like a finger stroking a thin crystal. The subdued sounds blended into the crystal vibration and created an atmosphere almost equal to the upper dimension."

M.P.
Escondido, California

"I 'saw' the area's inhabitants actually enter into crystal spires to recharge themselves as one would recharge a battery. This was how they renewed energy, not by sleep."

Name Withheld
Burbank, California

"In [the] Boynton Canyon Vortex, I found a place where I could see no one, hear no one; it was as if I were totally alone in the world, yet I knew I was surrounded by an infinite number of souls. I meditated . . . for an hour. I was awash with peace. Not once did an insect bother me, though I had no netting nor had I used insect repellent.

"As I was coming out of meditation, viewing the mysterious and wonderful sight in front of me, everything seemed to shimmer and glow. I saw a brief but moving view: to the left, a brilliant, unearthly flash of light; to the right, I saw long, long boats filled with people. The boats were moving quickly. I felt a sense of urgency."

Name Withheld
Columbia, Missouri

"I went into trance at Bell Rock and saw many beautiful light beings 'popping' through an amazingly blue sky, each transporting a crystal. Each came to rest on a grassy meadow which was located in the Sedona area. I was one of the light beings and a crystal was in my keeping. I looked up and saw others 'popping' through and finally a giant crystal 'popped' through and I knew the task was at once finished and just begun. We were now waiting for the people to come in the boats from across the sea to begin our task.

"My vision changed to a scene of building. Dark-haired, dark-skinned people were working along with the light beings to prepare a home, a place of safety, for the crystals beneath the Earth. The surface of the Earth was not to be disturbed, or at least as little as possible. Loving care was being exercised in this building. The dark-haired people had found homes in natural caves. Some of the light beings came to love the new land and the people so much they allowed themselves to be born into material existence, becoming caught in the cycle of karma. I was one of those."

Name Withheld
Topeka, Kansas

The following are excerpts of a three-page, single-spaced, typewritten letter I received from H.C.F. of Alhambra, California. She transcribed this extensively detailed message through automatic writing while in Boynton Canyon:

"Boynton Canyon is the center of the Inner City. Here is the purification center. Many beings from other planets return to earth to merge with us to help, to center, and to teach.

"When Lemuria sank into the Pacific, many had relocated. The healing center was transformed here. Caves were dug by use of crystals.

"This was a center for healing and rejuvenation. People of Lemuria traveled for years to attain the secrets of the crystals and the healers. Many beings, human and extraterrestrial, who were once residents of Mu, are now being drawn back to the area for healing, rejuvenation, and guidance.

"This will be the center of the coming age. Once again, the people of Mu will switch frequency and lead the populace to peace, harmony, and a high spirituality. The guidance is being received in many ways.

"What most beings, especially earth beings, do is restrict the growth process. The people of Mu learned to expand those lessons with 'freedom,' the process of allowing each spirit to grow in any and all directions. Each must find their own center of their heart, of their spirit, and then follow it, while allowing everyone around them to follow their own heart.

"What happened since Mu was destroyed was the process of everyone having to conform, to believe the same, to follow someone else's spirit. How can someone believe or follow when they have no heart or spirit in the matter? There is a beauty in difference and this should be expanded, not controlled.

"Many do not know how to handle freedom. This must be taught, for freedom without responsibility is not freedom, but a worse jail of the soul than restriction. The beauty of freedom is the ability to love unconditionally.

"Don't mourn the end of a civilization; celebrate the beginning of a new age, an age that not only allows change and difference but encourages it.

"You ask of peace . . . peace is everywhere, for it is contained in the soul of each of us. Most look for the physical peace of the outside world, like the peace and serenity of Boynton Canyon. But the same peace and serenity is within each being. One must start from the heart.

"The Inner City is now used as a monitoring center of earth. The large crystal controls all activity. The red earth carries the healing energies of the crystal to all who seek it. Each is drawn to the spot of frequency closest to their own.

"The maze of tunnels covers the whole area. The whole valley is a vortex, for the crystals are moved and worked in all areas. The works of the Inner City use the crystals to heal the earth and those upon it. As the crystals are used, so they in turn are energized . . . sort of a mutual exchange.

"Most rituals of healing are done in the Boynton Canyon area. Communications are most successful at Bell Rock. Any of the vortexes may be used for assistance, but results are stronger in certain areas.

One can ask for assistance from the beings of the Inner City.

"Remember to always acknowledge the healing or communications came from God or from the God-essence of oneself."

CHAPTER 4

"THE LOST CONTINENT OF MU"

by Gregory Frazier

The Garden of Eden was not in Asia but on a now sunken continent in the Pacific Ocean. The Biblical story of creation—the epic of the seven days and the seven nights—came first not from the peoples of the Nile or of the Euphrates Valley but from this now submerged continent, Mu—"the Motherland of Man."

Thus Colonel James Churchward (1852–1936) began the first in a series of five books about the ancient and mysterious sunken land of the Pacific, *The Lost Continent of Mu*.

In these books, Churchward claimed to have not only found the keys to unlock the mystery of the origin of man but to have traced his ancient migrations to the four corners of the earth. Today there are those who believe that the Lemurian migrations eventually led to the American

Southwest and the beautiful red-rock country surrounding present-day Sedona.

The name "Lemuria" was coined by scientists to describe the sunken mid-Pacific continent that was the original habitat of a far-ranging species of ape-like quadrupeds called lemurs. All ancient writings, however, refer to the lost continent as "Mu."

Churchward also pointed out some fascinating parallels connecting the inhabitants of Mu and certain Southwest Indian tribes. According to Churchward, these tribes are direct descendants of ancient Lemurians.

"I am not a professional archaeologist," Churchward wrote, "but I love the ancient, and for over fifty years, have been diligent in the study of it."

Born into an aristocratic Devonshire family, Churchward was educated at Oxford and served in India as a colonel of a regiment of Bengal Lancers. At various times during his adventurous career, the tall, dashing Englishman was an explorer, big-game hunter, angler, inventor, tea planter, painter, civil engineer, and raconteur. He was also a Mason and reincarnationist who practiced telepathy and trance-travel to former incarnations. Eventually, he settled in the United States, where he made—and later lost—a fortune in the steel business.

As a young man serving in India as a double agent for British Intelligence, he had occasion to visit a monastery. There he met an old rishi, whom he described as a "great master, the last surviving member of the ancient Naacal priesthood."

The rishi eventually led Churchward to a hidden cave and a cache of ages-old clay tablets. The tablets were written in Naacal, the rishi explained, the oldest language of man. They told of the geology, history and religion of Mu the Motherland, and its cataclysmic destruction over 12,000 years earlier.

"He taught me how to learn to read ancient writings and inscriptions," Churchward wrote in *The Children of Mu*. "It was a hobby of his and mine also."

Churchward wrote the first edition of *The Lost Continent of Mu* on the basis of his interpretation of the Naacal tablets. He later revised the book after interpreting another series of 12,000-year-old tablets discovered, beginning in 1921 by mineralogist William Niven in the Valley of Mexico. Together, the Naacal and Niven tablets provided the foundation of Churchward's hypothesis.

According to Churchward and other Mu historians, Mu comprised an area of some 180,000 square miles. The Pacific islands are believed to be Lemurian mountain tops. When devastating earthquakes sank Lemuria on Friday the 13th day of Zac, 64 million souls were drowned, an end to 200 millennia of development.

Wishar S. Cervé, in his book *Lemuria—The Lost Continent of the Pacific* described the typical Lemurian as a tall, well-muscled vegetarian who was far advanced mentally and spiritually. In the center of a high forehead was a growth about the size of a walnut. This "third eye" was actually the Lemurian's sixth sense organ. Through it, he could see, hear, feel, and communicate over long distances. He was also capable of communicating with animals, and could "see" into the fourth dimension.

The Lemurians possessed powerful magnetic stones or crystals, found in volcanic areas, which radiated energy and light. These crystals had the strange ability to repel water and were used to power the boats which ultimately brought the Lemurians to North America.

Lemurian religion was based on fact, as opposed to faith, containing no sects, theologies, or dogma. All Lemurians were attuned to the Cosmic Mind or Consciousness, which permeates the universe.

Reincarnation, an established fact to the Lemurians, was the crux of their religion. "In the Sacred Writings of Mu," Churchward wrote, "we are told man's soul lives on until finally it reaches the source of its origin."

About 70,000 years before the destruction of Mu, a colonial movement began sending groups of migrations westward to Asia and eastward to South, Central, and North America. The first of these eastern migrations led to approximately the present state of Nevada at a time preceding the rising of our western mountain ranges.

As evidence of the Lemurian presence in the Southwest, Churchward offers geographic, linguistic, symbolic, and religious data gathered from various [American] Indian tribes: the Nootka of British Columbia, the Mound Builders of the Southeast, the Pueblo Indians (Hopi and Zuni), and the Cliff Dwellers of the Southwest. The Cliff Dwellers were the last to arrive.

"Working inland from the Colorado River's mouth, they would first pass through Arizona, which state is full of their remains," Churchward explained. "Their old homes and remains show that they worked out on the Gila, Little Colorado, and Grand Rivers."

Montezuma Castle National Monument, an Arizona cliff dwelling, is located just a few miles from Sedona. Also nearby is the Tuzigoot National Monument, a stone pueblo where hundreds of Indians lived between 1100–1400 A.D. Were the inhabitants of these dwellings Lemurians or descendants of the Lemurians?

According to Churchward, there were at least four civilizations occupying Arizona and the Southwest *before* the Cliff Dwellers and the present-day [American] Indians. "It is quite possible that the actual Cliff Dwellers and the Pueblo Indians may be races that have descended from remnants that were saved during the raising of the mountains," he theorized. He points to their writings on boulders and cliffs which contain symbols similar to those found on the Naacal and Niven tablets.

"That the Cliff Dwellers came from Mu is certain," Churchward wrote, "for every one of their pictures that are used for guideposts contains a reference to Mu. In fact, the rock writings and pictures of the Cliff Dwellers, except those drawn for artistic effects, are permeated with references to Mu, both before and after her submersion. In addition to this, they invariably used the symbols that were in vogue in the Motherland."

Churchward investigated several interesting parallels between the Hopi and Zuni cultures and that of Lemuria. He believed that these [American] Indian tribes were highly developed and enlightened people at the time of their arrival in the Southwest.

"Various Pueblo traditions, their language, their sacred symbols, and other evidences *prove that the Pueblo Indians originally came to America from Mu*," (Note: The italics are Churchward's.)

Particularly fascinating is Quetzalcoatl, the bearded serpent, symbol of creation, which is common to the Pueblos, Mayans, Aztecs—and Lemurians. One of the Niven tablets, discovered at a grave site in Guerrero, Mexico, was interpreted by Churchward as follows: "Quetzalcoatl . . . called him, and his soul passed on to the region of darkness (submerged Mu) there to await the call from the great serpent for reincarnation." And this: "When Quetzalcoatl . . . calls—the eyes of those closed in sleep are opened, the time of their reincarnation has arrived. They answer the call of the Great Serpent and come forth into a new day."

Could Mu be the limbo of dead souls waiting for their moment of reincarnation?

Hopi legend would seem to support Churchward's hypothesis. The Hopis believe they originally came out of the west on bamboo rafts. Arriving at a wall of steep mountains, they climbed to the top and looked back; in the distance, they could see islands sinking. The continent of Mu consisted of one large and two smaller islands.

The Hopis are a deeply religious culture with many magic-oriented beliefs—as were the Lemurians. Beneath their dwellings, the Hopis dig kivas, underground rooms used for religious ceremonies. The Lemurians also used underground rooms for religious rites.

The indigenous people consider the Sedona red-rock country to be sacred ground; the home of the Great Spirit. Perhaps this is why so many people in search of enlightenment and inner peace come to this area, attracted, as it were, by some invisible force. Visitors from the ethereal plane are also said to linger here.

Amazing psychic occurrences have been reported as well: visions, telepathy, past-life regressions, precognitions, UFO sightings, poltergeist activity, enhanced automatic writing, spiritual healings, and other psychic phenomena.

An ancient Lemurian city is said to be buried beneath the Cococino sandstone. Powerful talisman-like crystals are thought to be hidden underground. (Coincidentally, the Navajo Indians believe that they emerged from underground.)

This testimony isn't surprising, considering that Sedona is one of the world's most powerful energy centers. Surrounding Sedona are four energy vortexes—two electric, one magnetic, and one electromagnetic—more than any other single spot on earth!

Unseen forces are constantly at work all around us. Every physical object on earth—organic and inorganic—gives off electromagnetic radiation. The effects of these unseen forces are little understood. What is understood, however, is that electromagnetic fields do affect living organisms. Metabolism, heart rate, body temperature, blood pressure, as well as the visual, aural, and tactile senses are affected by electromagnetism. Experiments with monkeys have shown, for example, that when the monkey's head is placed in an electromagnetic field tuned to alpha, its brain waves will begin to pulse in synchronization with the alpha rate.

In other words, truth and reality exist on many different levels. The parallels between ancient Lemuria and modern Sedona certainly deserve further investigation—on all levels. Given the awesome natural beauty of the Sedona redrock country, perhaps we should heed the rishi's parting words to the young Churchward:

"Go forth into the world, my son, and learn that which is written by nature. Nature is the great schoolhouse provided for man in which to learn. Nature does not theorize. Nature does not lie. Nature is truth personified. . . . Every rock has a tale written on its wrinkled and weathered face, and the tales are true. Every blade of grass, every leaf on tree, and shrub has a whisper for listening ears."

CHAPTER 5

"LEY LINES LINK SEDONA TO ALL EARTH'S POWER SPOTS"

by Kathie Dame-Glerum

In China, they are known as Dragon Currents, in Ireland as Fairy Paths, in the Americas as Serpent Power. The Aborigines in Australia refer to a "line of songs." And in England, the ley line systems are referred to simply as the Old Straight Track.

Ley lines are lines of natural magnetic currents—alignments of prehistoric sites and natural landmarks. A number of ley lines mark some extreme position of the sun or moon. Frequently, they are ancient roads or pathways, clearly visible from the air; sometimes they are only briefly visible as shadows or light paths.

Locating ley line energy was an ancient art not unlike that of dowsing with divining rods: a carefully taught science handed down through magicians, Druidic priests in the early mystery schools, and Chinese geomancers. The job of the geomancer was to interpret the earth in terms of the heavens, to detect currents and assess their influence on the land. Migrating birds, following a line of magnetic current, were often studied.

Ley lines are marked by giant earthworks and mounds in the American Midwest; by dirt roadways leading from Chaco Canyon, New Mexico, to Teotihuacan, Mexico; by a series of long, straight tracks emanating from Cuzco, the old Inca capital high in the Peruvian Andes, which is associated in local tradition with a primeval, godlike race; by lines crisscrossing the Nazca plains of Peru—lines with great astrological significance, oriented in such a way as to predict equinoxes and solstices. And they are marked by visible lines tying together every major religious site in Britain, from Stonehenge to the legendary Glastonbury Tor, home of King Arthur, Merlin, and the Holy Grail.

Every early Christian church was sited along the flow of ley line current, the great energy located directly beneath the tower [or steeple] to produce the strongest fusion of heaven and earth. The Dragon Currents of China mark all sacred paths and centers throughout that country. These currents are divided into those of yin and yang, positive and negative, the currents of the White Tiger and the Blue Dragon. The Chinese believe that the dragon pulse—the energy vortex—is at its peak where the yin of gently undulating country meets the yang of sharp rocks and peaks, particularly if this site is quiet and sheltered and secluded, as is much of Sedona.

Sedona is noted worldwide for its high concentration of active energy and power. The residents will often speak of "genies loci." Sedona spelled backward is "anodes": in an electrolytic cell, [it is] the positively charged electrode toward which the current flows; in an electron tube, the principal electrode for collecting electrons. Also, according to Webster's [history and etymology], "way up." Perhaps this is indeed what Sedona provides. It is the only spot on earth to contain four major vortexes within a few square miles.

A vortex is a high concentration of energy, a receiving station for direct influences; by definition, a state resembling a whirlpool. It is surrounded by grids—a similar energy field that is not yet centered—where ley lines share a common point of intersection.

The vortex areas have been likened to acupressure points on the body. In a similar manner, grids can be compared to the nervous system. At the point where these are concentrated, as in Sedona, emotions run high. Things happen at these points first—on the earth's body as well as on our own. Together, they form a sacred geometric pattern across the earth with universal repercussions.

Like attracts like; therefore, electrical vortexes will be connected via ley lines or electrical currents to other electrical vortexes. In Sedona, the Bell Rock and Airport Mesa Vortexes are connected to other major electrical vortexes on Mount Everest, Mount Ararat in Eastern Turkey, and Denali ([formerly called] Mount McKinley) in Alaska. The magnetic vortex at Cathedral Rock is connected to the major magnetic vortex of Glastonbury Tor in Britain, another recognized site of great regeneration.

As you meditate in any of the vortexes in the Sedona area, you are tying into a universal energy pattern of astounding magnitude and not just one particular energy facet. The key seems to lie in certain sound combinations reverberating throughout the universal ley line system: in humming, as reported by guides in certain chambers of the Great Pyramids; in the legendary song of the Sirens;

and in chanting heard by those who have remained quiet long enough while deep into Boynton Canyon. The healing circles of Dick Sutphen, held in Sedona, are extremely powerful: the vibrations of the "OM" chant combining with the human magnetism of the group and resounding in a universal spirit of love and healing physically felt.

The ley line system has always meant healing, the renewal of the life force. The lines themselves become animated at certain seasons of the year by a vital force, a rejuvenating influence that can be drawn through the earth. And the direction of its flow varies with the phases of the moon.

From time immemorial, ancient rites have been performed on the ley lines throughout the earth within arrangements of carved dots and stone circles to ensure the return of this force—from the druids of Britain and the Aborigines of Australia to the K'iche' (formerly spelled Quiche) Maya of South America. The Hopi use the lines as cables of mental communication. It is said that stone can be levitated by sound along the ley lines of magnetic intensity, the level of intensity altered by tone and pitch.

The late Dr. Wilhelm Reich in *The Discovery of the Orgone* proved the existence of this pure life force, which he called "orgone energy," by storing and channeling it to produce dramatic changes in the weather with the use of a simple apparatus. He felt, by using the ley line system, even space travel was possible with the flow of intergalactic currents of energy.

It seems only logical to believe that there was, long ago, a universal civilization with an advanced knowledge of science and magic: a magic based on numbers, which unified all the individual arts and sciences, customs, folklore, mythology, monuments, and cultures universally. It is a physical fact that the prehistoric sites fall into perfectly straight alignments when shown on a map. And all these sites were mathematically equated and built with extraordinary precision.

The actual key to all these ancient and natural sites seems to lie in numbers.

The vibrational force of the ley line/vortex/grid system in Sedona is the number seven. As Sedona is said to be built over an ancient Lemurian city, it is interesting to note that seven is also the number of Lemuria.

From the beginning of time, the mystical code of numbers and vibrations, translated into sound and light patterns, has been at the root of all ancient knowledge and belief. And the ley line/vortex/grid system has been the power by which it is transferred. There is a oneness to be felt with the universe that seems to come more easily in a vortex or healing circle in Sedona. And a responsibility to return that which is given—knowledge and spirit . . . and peace.

Another explanation for these power spots was put forth by C. W. Leadbeater, one of the early leaders of the Theosophical Society. In 1910, he authored a two-volume set of books titled *The Inner Life*. The books represent a general overview of the entire metaphysical belief structure. In a chapter about the work of the Masters, he explains that 1,900 years ago, the White Brotherhood sent a man upon a mission to establish magnetic centers in various countries:

> Objects of the nature of talismans were given to him, which he was to bury at these chosen spots, in order that the force which they radiated might prepare these places to be the centers of great events in the future.[1]

Another interesting quote from the same book:

> Masters frequently take advantage of special occasions and of places where there is some strong magnetic center. Where some holy man has lived and

died, or where some relics of such a person create a suitable atmosphere, they take advantage of such conditions and cause their own force to radiate along the channels which are already prepared. When some vast assemblage of pilgrims comes together in a receptive attitude, again they take advantage of the occasion by pouring their forces out upon the people through the channels by means of which they have been taught to expect help and blessing.[2]

Perhaps this explains the enormous psychic impact Sedona has on both the aware and the unaware and those who have attended Sedona Psychic Seminars there.

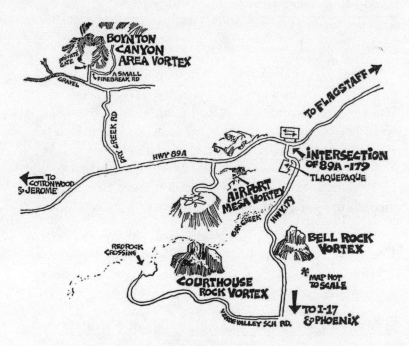

This map shows the placement of the vortexes in Sedona. The map is not to scale. Credit: Dick Sutphen

CHAPTER 6

VORTEX LOCATIONS AND WARNINGS

In this chapter, I will give you the exact locations of the four primary vortexes with detailed explanations of how to reach them. In addition, I will share with you some very important information you need to know before experiencing these very intense vibrational fields.

First, I want to make a very strong point about the spirituality of the vortex areas, especially the Boynton Canyon area. As you read in previous chapters, the area is considered sacred by the Yavapai. When you enter here, have the same respect you would as if you were entering a place of worship, for that's what it is. Even now, you may encounter American Indians here; they still travel from the cities and reservations to regularly observe their religious practices in the canyon. If you should see them worshipping in the area, please move quietly away so as not to disturb them. Don't stand around and gawk.

Because of all the recent development, especially at the mouth of Boynton Canyon, it has been increasingly difficult for the American Indians, especially the elders who are not as agile, to gain access to these sacred areas. Attempts are being made to improve access to the canyon. Supposedly, a new trail is now being constructed. We should support every effort to make access to the sacred areas easier for the indigenous people and to avoid disturbing them while we pursue our own worship and meditations.

Please be extremely respectful in every way while experiencing the vortex area; this includes taking out everything that you carry in, from cigarette butts to drink containers. I'm especially concerned about the ecology, but beyond that, you don't want to upset the spirits who reside here.

Also, remember that Arizona is rattlesnake country. Wear hiking boots, or even better, high-topped boots such as cowboy boots. The only problem with cowboy boots is that they are terrible for climbing if you plan to scale any of the higher areas. Extensive climbing is really unnecessary to experience any of the vortex areas, but you may want to climb just for the experience or for another view of the beautiful surrounding country. There is little concern about rattlesnakes in the winter months for they are hibernating, but as the weather becomes warmer, the risk of running into rattlesnakes becomes greater. In the spring, the snakes will often come out to warm themselves on the rocks; in the summer months, they can be a real problem. *Never* walk through grass where you don't have a full view of the surrounding ground—snakes will often be under rocks or brush. Make plenty of noise as you walk; this will give the snakes a chance to get out of your way. They don't want to confront you any more than you want to confront them.

In my years of exploring the Arizona desert areas, I've had at least 25 encounters with snakes, and I must stress the importance of being aware. Never, under any circumstances while climbing or moving through the rocks, place your hand in a position that you can't see. Climbers pulling themselves up the rocks have reached up to grab hold and have been struck in the hand, or worse yet, pulled themselves up to a ledge or shelf only to come face to face with a coiled snake.

It is best to work with someone else in the vortex areas in the warmer months because of the snakes. Take along a blanket or pad to sit or lie on if you plan to explore in an altered state of consciousness. Place it in an open area away from piles of rocks and underbrush. While one person is in a trance, the other can watch over them. They can also be of assistance, as I'll describe later.

Also, never sleep in a sleeping bag on the open ground anywhere in Arizona. If you plan to camp, bring along a closed tent or a cot that will keep you off the ground. Rattlesnakes are known to slither down into a sleeping bag to share the warmth generated by the inhabitant's body heat. All will be fine until you desire to crawl out of the bag, which might upset the snake.

Please don't allow the discussion of rattlesnakes and scorpions to keep you from experiencing the vortex areas or to do so in a paranoid state. If you keep in mind what I've told you, your chances of encountering a snake are extremely rare. I just don't want you blundering across the Arizona landscape as if you were in a park in the city. Be aware that the desert is the snakes' home, not yours.

If you should encounter a coiled snake rattling its tail, freeze immediately; judge the situation, and if appropriate, back slowly away. The snake is capable of striking only its own length, but five-foot rattlers aren't rare in this area. If you are struck get away instantly, for a rattler will strike again and again as long as its prey is within reach, and the first strike carries only a small amount of venom in comparison to the second, when the snake's system is fully pumping the poison.

If you are bitten, keep the bite above your heart area. Get to a hospital or emergency care center immediately.

Although nocturnal, scorpions are another consideration in Arizona. While snakes will usually attempt to avoid you, scorpions will rush to meet you. Experts claim they can see little more than light and dark, so they determine the approach of prey by ground vibrations.

A scorpion bite is not deadly for most people, but it is painful and can make you sick. Scorpions usually hide under rocks, behind tree bark, or between the cracks in rocks. If you pick up a rock with a scorpion on the bottom, it will most likely crawl up on your hand. Don't sit on rocks with open cracks. Scorpions are attracted to water, so even in a hotel room, be careful when picking up a wet swimsuit or towel. Don't walk around barefoot. Old Arizona programming, resulting from years as a Scottsdale resident, has me shake out my shoes before putting them on when visiting Sedona.

Another warning to be considered is in regard to inner voices that empathic people are known to have experienced in the vortex areas. A good friend, who knows the Boynton Canyon area like the back of his hand, found himself following the voices. He climbed high up into the rocks and crevices, only to get himself into a position that required every bit of climbing skill he possessed to get himself safely down. The slightest slip and he could have fallen to his death.

Seminar participant J.C.H. of Lynn, Massachusetts, had a similar experience when he went to the Airport Mesa Vortex late one night:

"When I was first told about Sedona, it came to mind that a certain gift should be brought . . . a piece of jade. I went to the Airport Mesa; it was around ten o'clock at night and pitch black. Parking my car and grabbing my flashlight, I started the climb up.

"After walking for a few minutes, a voice said to me, 'Turn off the light, you will not need it.' So I did as I was instructed. It was dark, but I could see with no problem at all and continued to climb.

"Several times I heard rocks clattering, as if a person had stepped and moved a rock in doing so. Being an avid outdoorsman, I knew it was not an animal—it was a two-legged creature, not a four-legged one. And, as I stated earlier, I could see in the dark.

"Eventually, I reached the top and walked to the edge, which I could see with no problem. It was at the very top of the mesa where I knew I was supposed to leave the jade. But I wanted to be absolutely sure. So I said, 'I will leave it tomorrow after going to the Courthouse and Boynton Canyon Vortexes.' (Note: He had already been to the Bell Rock Vortex earlier.)

"It was like a voice saying, 'No, leave it here.' I said, 'No, tomorrow,' and continued down the mesa.

"I stepped on a rock, and it was as though it just jumped out from under my right foot. Well, needless to say, I fell and banged my left knee. And a voice said, 'Leave the jade.' I said, 'No, I'll leave it tomorrow.'

"The reason I wanted to hold onto the jade is that I wanted to go to the other vortexes and see if I got a stronger inclination to leave the jade someplace else.

"After a few minutes of pain—I didn't swear or cuss—I got up and continued. I brushed a cactus and got quite a few thorns in my left leg. And again, a voice said, 'Leave the jade.' Again, I said, 'No, I'll leave it tomorrow.'

"A few minutes later, something stopped me. Something just wasn't right. I looked again and it looked as though I were at the edge of a rim. I turned on my flashlight, and sure enough, I was on the edge of a rim with a parking lot in front of me. If I had continued without stopping, I would have fallen about eight feet."

Remember, spirits can be of lower as well as higher vibrations. Whenever you contact spirit voices in meditation, automatic writing, self-hypnosis, or any other altered state, use your own intuition in evaluating what they have to say. In general, your guides or good spirits do just that— they "guide" you. If you ever encounter voices or written suggestions demanding that you do something, beware! Not all entities are working in your best interests. Trust your own feelings and good sense as to whether you should do as they suggest.

As in these two cases, voices telling you to climb to a dangerous or inaccessible location (even with the "promise" of some kind of reward or discovery), or to climb a mountain in the dark, or do anything that you would ordinarily consider unsafe to do, or that could be physically, mentally, or emotionally destructive, are probably of a malevolent nature. Ignore them. And, as an added protection, imagine yourself surrounded with the white God light. Don't let the experiences override common sense. Even if you know the back country, Arizona is unique and you need considerable survival skills and adequate water and supplies to explore safely.

There are many ancient Indian caves in the area, and if you dig in any of these, you are subject to a fine of several thousand dollars and a term in prison. There are also very stringent laws about digging up any of the cactuses or plants on park land and public property. I also feel it is very bad luck to remove any rocks from the vortex areas without permission of the spirits, attained while in meditation.

THE VORTEX LOCATIONS

After describing the exact locations of the vortexes, I'll tell you my own ways of testing the energy and activating and expanding upon it for your own subjective explorations. I'll begin all my directions from the center of Sedona at the junction of Highways 89A and 179. Directions are well marked at the intersection. If you follow 89A toward Flagstaff, you'll drive up the switchbacks through Oak Creek Canyon. This is one of the most beautiful drives on earth, although no major vortex areas are located in this direction. If you follow 89A west toward Cottonwood and Jerome, you are moving in the proper direction for the Airport Mesa Vortex and the Boynton Canyon Area Vortex. All visitors will want to make the trip to Jerome, which takes about 40 minutes. This is the largest ghost town in the country and once was a thriving mining area. Today, many craftsmen have moved back there, repairing some of the deteriorating homes and have opened shops and restaurants.

If you take Highway 179 out of town, it will lead you past Tlaquepaque, the beautiful Spanish Colonial shopping and craft center. Past Tlaquepaque and on out 179 toward Black Canyon Freeway, which is Interstate 17, you'll come to the Bell Rock Vortex and the turnoff to the Courthouse Rock Vortex. (Note: There is some confusion between Courthouse

[Rock] and Cathedral Rock on some maps. On the old maps, the vortex area is called Courthouse Rock, so that's the name I'll use in this book.)

I will give you the mileage points as they register on your car's odometer, but remember that some odometers may register a little differently, depending upon the size of your tires, so keep this variant in mind when following these instructions.

I've included a little map of the area to make finding the vortexes much easier, but a map is not necessary if you follow these directions exactly. Everything I'll relate is accurate at the time of this printing, and although the vortexes and the main roads won't change, some road signs, change in property ownership, and new constructions can alter circumstances.

For instance, you used to be able to drive in quite close to most of the vortexes, but recently the National Park Service has put up fences blocking the roads into these areas and is constructing parking lots, probably because of the increasing amount of visitors to these spiritual locations. So although you'll have to walk farther to get to the vortexes, parking should be less of a problem than it has been in the past.

Where you used to be able to drive up to the base of Bell Rock, now you have to stop about one-eighth of a mile away. At Red Rock Crossing, near Courthouse Rock, you'll have to hike about half a mile. Two new parking lots are there now.

Before I describe the exact locations of the four primary vortexes, let me just reiterate the types of positive vortexes found in Sedona and the kind of energy they radiate. Positive vortexes are charged in one of three ways:

- **Electric:** These are "yang," charged with the male force. When you enter the vibrational field or frequency, you will become charged emotionally and physically. The energy will stimulate and elevate consciousness. It is also ideal to eliminate depression. Some people consider an electrical vortex to be a strain on someone with high blood pressure or heart problems.

- **Magnetic**: These are "yin," charged with the female force. When you enter the vibrational field or frequency, you can expect to open psychically, becoming much more perceptive, for the effects are primarily on the subconscious mind.

- **Electromagnetic**: These vortexes are a combination of electrical and magnetic, or a combination of the yin-yang forces, resulting in a perfect state of balance. When you enter the vibrational field or frequency, you can expect an expansion and elevation of consciousness. This energy is ideal to stimulate past-life memories and psychic activities.

Bell Rock (An Electric Vortex). Location: From the inter-section of Highways 89A and 179, drive out of Sedona on 179 toward Black Canyon Freeway, which is Interstate 17. Drive 5.1 miles on 179; on the left-hand side of the road is Bell Rock. It is impossible to miss; it is a huge bell-shaped red rock that sits just off the highway on your left.

This is purported to be a beacon vortex; it is said that the energy emits from the base and out the top, extending miles into the air. This may explain why there have been so many UFO sightings above Bell Rock over the years. Those desiring to experience the energy of Bell Rock Vortex would have to be right at, or up on, the base. Because it is electric, being within the frequency should stimulate conscious-ness. Due to the beacon-like quality, psychics report that the location is excellent for communication with higher forms of life.

Airport Mesa (An Electric Vortex). Location: From the intersection of Highways 89A and 179, drive 1.1 miles toward Cottonwood and turn left at Airport Road. Go up Airport Road four-tenths of a mile. The "Cattle Guard" sign that used to be there is gone, but on the right side of the road is a sign saying "Rainbow Ray Focus." Not far away is a pull-off area on the right. The trail to the vortex is on your left, about halfway between the sign and the pull-off area. There are a couple of rough trails that lead up the hill.

Please be aware that unless your car is completely off the road, it will be towed away, and there is only enough room for a few cars to pull off. So if other people are in the [pull-off] area, park your car and walk up to the area.

Once you've come to the top of the hill, you'll walk down into the vortex area. It is approximately half a block long and stops at a cliff that looks down on the valley below. This is the vortex I wrote about in one of my books. Because it is electric in nature, it can be expected to charge you emo-tionally and physically while also elevating consciousness.

Courthouse Rock (A Magnetic Vortex). (Note: Also called Cathedral Rock on some maps.) Location: From the intersection of Highways 89A and 179, drive out of Sedona on 179 toward Black Canyon Freeway, which is Interstate 17. You'll come to the Village of Oak Creek, and when your odometer reads 7.2 miles, turn right on Verde Valley School Road. Continue for another 3.2 miles and you'll see Court-house Rock, the huge rock formation on your right, several blocks from the road. This is the closest you can get to the rock without a four-wheel-drive vehicle. And, although Courthouse Rock is the most photographed rock formation in the area, this view is the least desirable. If you want to view it at its best, continue down Verde Valley School Road for another 2.1 miles until the road dead-ends into Oak Creek. You can also walk in from this point, which is more scenic but is a greater distance.

The vortex energy emanations are said to extend from Courthouse Rock to about 500 yards around the base. Because it is magnetic in nature, you can expect the activation of your subconscious mind, becoming more psychic, and stimulating forgotten memories, past lives, and so on.

Because the Courthouse is "yin" charged, some people are concerned that it emits negative energy. On one level, yin denotes negative, but this certainly is not the kind of negativity you would experience in a negative vortex area such as the Bermuda Triangle. The yin energy of Courthouse Rock could be likened to the positive and negative energy in an automobile battery. A battery consists of alternating positive- and negative-charged plates. It is the alternating interaction of the two that generates the energy that you use to start your car and power the electrical components. The negative plate isn't "bad," any more than the positive plate is "good." All structures require the yin-yang interaction to exist. Human beings are also structures.

Boynton Canyon Area (An Electromagnetic Vortex). Location: From the intersection of Highways 89A and 179, drive toward Cottonwood, Arizona, 3.2 miles, until you come to Dry Creek Road on the right. Turn right and proceed down Dry Creek Road another 2.9 miles until the road forks. At this point, turn left following the signs directing you toward

Boynton Pass; go another 1.6 miles until the road forks again. Turn right following the Boynton Canyon sign. About four-tenths of a mile down this road on the right is a U.S. Forestry Service parking area. Pull in and park, or park along the road.

If, instead of parking there, you had driven another one-tenth of a mile down the road, you would have come to the gate of a private resort. At this printing, the resort is called Enchantment, but there have been several owners and the name may change. Since Boynton Canyon is considered the home of the Great Mother and sacred ground to the Yavapai, I question whether any commercial venture will ever be successful there.

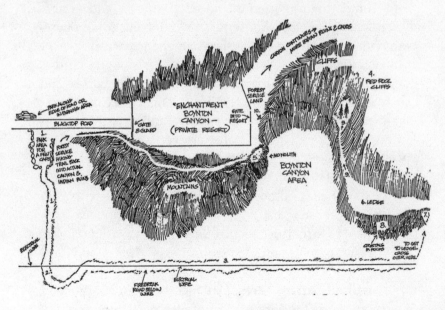

This map shows Boynton Canyon. Credit: Dick Sutphen

This 70-acre resort development blocks the direct entrance to Boynton Canyon, but the Forestry Service has cut a hiking trail that edges the property and allows you to hike back into the canyon.

The vortex energy appears to be centered on a monolith-like section of the mountain. (Note: See the map on page 68. The appearance of a monolith is more apparent from the back side.) So you can enjoy the vortex energy in Boynton Canyon or in the canyon area on the other side of the mountain. I would suggest that you plan to spend the whole day there and explore both sides.

Boynton Canyon: Follow the Forest Service signs back into the canyon. As you reach the area parallel to the back gate of the resort property, you'll see a huge cavelike opening high in the red-rock wall. Indian ruins remain in this overhang. (Note: #10 on the map.) Don't miss it if you are capable of a moderate climb. My five-year-old son Hunter did it on his own with very little help. Upon reaching the overhang, you'll find the standing adobe walls of the Indians' living quarters. This is a wonderful place to meditate.

If you hike deeper into Boynton Canyon, there are plenty of remote places to meditate off the trail and alongside the creek bed.

Boynton Canyon Area: To get to the area on the other side of the canyon, look at the map and follow the numbered instructions, which correspond to points on the map.

1. Proceed through the parking area and down the trail a few blocks until you come to an electrical line, which is just a wire in the sky.

2. Turn left and follow the wire, which is above the firebreak road. You can follow it as far as you want to go into the canyon area. It's a several-block walk.

3. By the time you've walked about a half mile down the firebreak road, off to your left you will begin to see smooth, sheer red-rock walls ascending hundreds of feet into the air.

4. You can leave the firebreak road and hike back into the canyon area as far as you want, but you'll have to make your way through the scrub, high-desert growth, which takes time.

5. Although the huge monolith-like section of the mountain at the back of the canyon area is said to be the source of the energy, there is so much energy that you don't have to be that close to the source to receive the benefits. I would suggest that you stay on the firebreak road until you are directly opposite the canyon area you desire to explore. By so doing, you'll avoid the extra effort of crossing excess scrub-desert terrain.

6. This ledge is one of my favorite meditation places.

7. To get to the ledge (unless you're a real mountain climber), you must climb up and cross over to the ledge where the land slopes up to meet it.

8. Directly below the ledge is an area where you can find an abundance of crystals in the rocks (if they haven't been chipped out—a bad-karma thing to do).

9. There is a thin trail beyond the ledge that leads to some beautiful meditation areas high up on the cliffs. There are trees in this upper area. If you decide to follow this trail, be very careful; it's a long way down.

The Boynton Canyon Vortex is my favorite of the Sedona area vortexes. You don't even have to be psychically sensitive to experience the tremendous power here. This is also the largest vortex in the area, with energy emitting from the ground for several miles in every direction. Because the area is electromagnetic, it is perfectly balanced and will expand and elevate consciousness. It should stimulate all subconscious memories (past lives) and your psychic abilities should be greatly enhanced here.

MEDICINE WHEELS

As you explore the vortex areas, you will probably see medicine wheels built by those who came before you. These are rocks forming a wheel shape or possibly an altar. The site will have been used for meditation and/or rituals. Generally, the wheel depicts the total universe and the sacred way that all creation balances. It is a tool used to gain wisdom, guidance, and growth from external sources. The wheel teaches gentle dealing and respect for nature and its creatures and peoples. It also teaches one to sing the song of the world, to become whole and to be one with the universe. If you choose to meditate at one of these sites, you may tap into energy that others have generated. This could be very positive and loving energy or chaotic and confused energy, depending upon who constructed and used the wheel. Please be respectful of the medicine wheels you encounter. I'll add that the Forest Service asks you not to build any new ones.

CHAPTER 7

VORTEX EXPERIMENTS AND MEDITATIONS

You now have the four locations. And before I go into testing the energy and working in an altered state of consciousness, let me give you another tip that may very well make your vortex journey much more enjoyable. As with any outside location, especially in warm months, the vortexes will have some bugs and flies. Since you will be attempting to meditate or induce self-hypnosis, you'll need to be able to totally focus your attention upon subjective input without distractions, so bring a good insect repellent or some cheese-cloth or fine netting to place over your body while in trance.

Now, let's discuss how to test, activate, and expand the vortex energy to maximize the psychic potential of your vortex experience. First, if you conduct your subjective explorations in an altered state of consciousness, even if it is only a very light altered state, you are sure to be more successful, for you have easier access to subconscious awareness and memories when you are in alpha or theta brain levels.

A deeper trance will assist you in accessing the higher self or superconscious mind. This is certainly most desirable for contacting the other side or higher forms of life.

I'm sure most people interested in this book have already developed their own altered-state techniques, and if so, use what you are familiar with. If you are new to using an altered state of consciousness, which means meditation or self-hypnosis, simply follow these easy instructions:

To begin, make yourself comfortable in a sitting or prone position, and then take at least 10 very deep breaths. This yoga breathing technique has you take a very deep breath in and then hold it as long as possible. Then let the breath out slowly through slightly parted teeth. This allows you to retain moisture in your mouth and thus be more comfortable. When you think the breath is all the way out, contract your stomach muscles and force the breath farther and farther out. Then breathe in and repeat the process. When you inhale using this technique, your diaphragm cuts in even before your lungs and it is very relaxing. So take at least 10 of these deep breaths—even more if you need them to calm down. While doing your deep breathing, begin to quiet your mind and focus your attention strictly upon the breathing process. You want to allow the quietness of spirit to begin to come in.

Next, mentally begin to relax your body one part at a time, beginning with your feet and moving up your legs into your hands, forearms, and upper arms. Then relax the base of your spine and move the relaxing power up your spine and into the back of your neck and shoulder muscles. The relaxing power is then able to move up your neck into your scalp and drain down into your facial muscles. As you think about each part of your body relaxing, play the role, play the part, and really feel the relaxing sensations coming into your body.

The next step is to imagine a beam of bright white light coming down from above and beginning to flow through your body and mind. This is the white God light of protection. Make this image real and create the light with the unlimited power of your mind. Next, imagine the light concentrating around your heart area and then emerging from your heart area to surround your body with a protective magnetic aura of God light. Personally, I also like to recite the following invocation of protection while I'm surrounding myself in this spiritual aura:

> To Thee, God, be the kingdom and the power and the glory unto the ages of ages . . . Amen. I seek Thy protection from all things seen and unseen, all forces and all elements. In Thy divine name, I open to the light. I offer my body, my mind, and my spirit to the light. Let Thy divine will and mine be as one. I seek to expand the light within and I seek a tranquil mind and harmony with Thy divine law. I thank Thee in advance for the unfolding visions, spiritual awareness, and healing that await me. As it is above, so it is below. I ask these things in Thy name. I beseech it, and I mark it . . . and so it is.

Once the protection is complete, imagine yourself going down into a peaceful meditative state while you slowly count backward from 50 to one. While you are counting, vividly fantasize yourself climbing from the top of one of the beautiful red rocks slowly and safely down to the bottom. When you reach the number one, you will be in an altered state of consciousness.

Of course, the more you use an altered state, the more conditioned you become, and the better you are conditioned, the more likely you will be to have vivid experiences in the vortex area.

Once you are ready to awaken, all you have to do is count yourself up from one to five and say the words, "wide awake, wide awake."

Now, let's talk about how to experience the vortex energy while in an altered state. Once you've completed the count-down, slowly raise your hands, palms down, a few inches above the earth, and attempt to feel the energy.

Your mind must be relaxed and focused only on the feelings in your hands. Many people report great tingling in their hands, or that they begin to feel lighter and lighter, which is the energy pushing up out of the ground.

If you're on the edge of the vortex, hold your hands palms out toward the vortex area, and again, feel the energy. Then reverse the direction, palms away from the vortex area, and you'll feel much less energy. This experiment will work best if you're sitting at the top of the Airport Mesa Vortex before entering the actual vortex area. It will also work if you remain a distance from Bell Rock or Courthouse Rock. There is simply too much energy coming up out of the ground for miles around Boynton Canyon for this experiment to work well. You'll feel the energy no matter what direction you face.

Now, here are some additional experiments that for many, greatly increase and expand the energy. The first is with a crystal, or crystal pendulum, which is readily available from most metaphysical bookstores. Go into an altered state with the crystal on your third-eye area, in the center of your forehead. Conduct the experiments I've already described, or use it to open for psychic impressions or to ask to receive past-life information. I'll explain more about how to do this shortly. Another variation of this technique is to place the crystal on your psychic center acupressure point. This point can be easily found by running your finger down the center of your chest until you come to the bottom of your rib cage.

The point where the bone ends is the psychic center. Again, conduct the experiments or seek subjective input.

Crystals amplify body energy and thoughts. Many people use them to focus their energy. Crystals create power and clarity in thinking, and because the vortex opens you psychically and stimulates the subconscious, you can expect some vivid experiences. The crystal will also amplify the energy of the vortex.

Two variations of these experiments are to use a small pyramid or a small vortex rock in exactly the same manner as I've described with the crystals. Because we all differ vibrationally, not everyone will experience the same things—each person will have unique results with different techniques in the vortexes.

I've had people tell me that they have had their most vivid experiences when in the vortex area during a full moon or at the time of the new moon. Recent medical studies have shown that both these phases of the moon have a profound and measurable effect upon a great many people. Again, though, the effect can be negative as well as positive, so the energy of the vortex could exaggerate the negativity.

As is often the case when exploring astral projection, some people exploring vortex energy prefer to remove their clothes and all jewelry, and then lie down with their heads facing north. You'll have to judge the appropriateness of this technique for yourself. If you do desire to explore it, I'd suggest you find a secluded place in the Boynton Canyon area. Because Boynton Canyon is so large, you are less likely to be observed there by others.

I should probably also mention that some who have made love in the vortex have reported that it was spectacular—a merging of their energy on a spiritual level. If you and your partner decide to explore this potential in a spiritual place such as Boynton Canyon, I hope you will approach it as a spiritual experience rather than a lustful one. You are definitely dealing with spiritual forces and intense energy that you don't want amplified in the wrong way.

You may also wish to explore any psychic methodology you are already familiar with, such as the I Ching, Tarot cards, working with a pendulum, or automatic writing while in the vortex. I've personally experienced my most powerful response to automatic writing in the Airport Mesa Vortex. I've simply gone into an altered state of consciousness with a pencil and large notepad in my lap. I've then asked the spirits of the vortex to guide my hand and relate information that would be of interest or useful to me. Try it, even if you're not used to automatic writing. If you contact the vortex spirits, you will most likely contact American Indian entities. You can also call out to your own guides or highly evolved and loving entities who mean you well to guide your hand.

Because of Bell Rock's beacon-like quality, it is excellent for attempting to contact higher forms of life, especially in automatic writing, as well as possible communication with extraterrestrials.

There are various ways to perceive subjective input while in an altered state. Once you have completed the body relaxation, the protection invocation, and the countdown, I would suggest that you attempt to open for psychic input by asking for visions or conceptual input that would be of value for you to experience at this time. My own technique is very simple. I silently call out in my mind with the following invocation:

Once more I call out to the positive powers of the universe, to my guides and Masters and those who share my energy. I am now open to receive positive information that will assist me in learning what I most need to know to evolve spiritually. I seek awareness as to my purpose and mission upon the earth plane.

I seek your guidance and I seek a tranquil mind. I ask
this, I beseech it, and mark it . . . and so it is.

Once you've completed the invocation, become very
quiet inside. If any outside thoughts come into your mind,
brush them aside and be open to visual impressions, your
inner voices, and your thoughts. Sometimes, the most valuable awareness will simply come in the form of your own
thoughts, which in reality may be directed by your guides.
You may fall asleep and dream, which just might be what is
most valuable for you at the time.

When you are ready to return to full beta consciousness,
count yourself up from one to five and be sure to be very
quiet upon opening your eyes. Have a pen and paper by your
side or a tape recorder with blank tape so you can make written or verbal notes about what you have experienced. Psychic impressions and regression experiences are like dreams:
they fade quickly away once you are fully awake. So make
key notes immediately, and be sure to instruct others not to
disturb you when you awaken until you speak to them.

It is also fascinating to attempt a past-life regression
while in an altered state. Again, once you have completed
the body relaxation, the protection invocation, and the
countdown, I would suggest that you then use an invocation
similar to mine:

In the memory banks of my subconscious mind is
a memory of everything I have ever experienced.
Every thought, every action, every deed is recorded
from this life I am now living and from all my past
lives. I now desire to experience the memories and
impressions of a past life that would be of value for
me to explore at this time. I ask that you guide me
and remain with me as I re-explore my own past. I
ask it, I beseech it, and I mark it . . . and so it is.

79

Once this is completed, count slowly backward from five to one, and be open for any visual or mental impressions that begin to come in. And be fully aware that you are your own guide. You can simply ask questions about what you are receiving to change the input or to seek greater awareness of that which you don't understand. When you are finished, count yourself up from one to five.

Now, let me give you a tip that may prove extremely valuable. Often when people are exploring in an altered state, they tend to "trip out." Tripping is usually a problem encountered by well-conditioned subjects. You don't go to sleep, but you "trip away" and do not remember anything upon awakening. There are several ways to solve tripping, but the most effective is simply to verbally relate everything you are experiencing. This will not bring you out of trance. In fact, when I'm hypnotizing and regressing a subject, I ask them to verbalize their perceptions. By speaking aloud, you keep yourself from drifting off, and it may allow your partner to ask you questions. You can certainly try this as an experiment as long as you are inducing your own altered state. Please don't allow anyone but a trained hypnotist to hypnotize you. Although chances are that nothing negative will happen, with deep-level subjects, situations can occur that would panic an amateur while a trained hypnotist would handle it easily. If you're inducing your own trance, you can also easily awaken yourself if you don't like what you are receiving.

Once you have completed the body relaxation, the protective invocation, and the countdown, you can use an altered state of consciousness to tap the energies of the vortexes for healing or to send the healing energies to someone you know who is in need. Or you can visualize the person you desire to see healed, sending the healing energy to them to use as they see fit.

Here is an incantation I like to use:

I call out to the positive powers of the universe, to my guides and Masters and those who share my energy. I ask your assistance in healing my physical body and mind. I ask that you combine your energy with the energy of this vortex to heal me now. I am open to healing . . . I am healing . . . I am healed. I ask it, I beseech it, and I mark it . . . and so it is.

Now, in your mind, draw down the light from above— the universal life energy, the healing energy—and see it as an iridescent, shimmering blue light. Feel the light filling your body to overflowing with the healing power. Make this fantasy very, very vivid. Then imagine the healing energy emitting from the ground. Feel it combining with the light from above and then begin to imagine, very vividly, that you are healed. See yourself in your mind as healed. And as you imagine this, chant a mantra silently in your mind, or speak it aloud: "I am healing . . . I am healed . . . I am healing . . . I am healed." Repeat it over and over, and believe that you are healed. Continue this for at least 20 minutes while imagining the healing is taking place.

A variation of this technique is to direct the healing energy into your hands until you actually feel them heating up. If you direct the energy properly, they will heat up, and when they feel as though they are on fire, place them on the area of your body that you desire to have healed. Or you can, at this time, place your hands on someone else to heal them.

Now, I'm going to get more esoteric. I feel that it is possible to generate even more energy and power by invoking positive ancient powers. And my choice is the pentagram or pentacle—the five-pointed star, a symbol of ceremonial white magic.

The pentacle is the star of man. Five is the number of man, and the star has the meaning of five. The horizontal line is upheld by the soul, or the divine principle. This number denotes change and versatility. It is man reaching out through his five senses for experience. In ancient scriptures, it often pertains to the senses or to the planes of manifestation. And, the pentacle symbolizes spirit and the positive forces struggling against the forces of darkness.

For centuries, magicians have used the pentacle as a seal to prevent evil spirits from entering. If the star is used right side up, it invokes the positive powers. If used upside down, it symbolizes the elements dominating and is the pentacle of black magic.

In the vortexes, some people prefer to work within a pentacle. You can draw it in the dirt, form the pentacle with stones, or, as some prefer, use cornmeal to form the lines. Be sure to draw it with unbroken lines by making five connecting strokes.

Then stand, sit, or lie within the pentacle, facing the single top point. If you plan to lie down, face the top point to the north and lie with your head also facing north. Make sure the pentacle is large enough to encompass your entire body. Remain within the pentacle during all your explorations.

Some who are into ritual or ceremonial magic will use the ancient incantations, but you'll have to conduct this study on your own. It requires considerable investigation and awareness before invoking such power. Obviously, there are hundreds of variations of the techniques I've discussed and I hope you'll experiment on your own.

I believe you now have the general information you need to explore the Sedona energy vortexes. I realize I have gone to great lengths in cautioning visitors to the vortexes about the hazards—environmental, spiritual, emotional, and physical—and in stressing the spirituality of the area. It is because I truly believe Sedona is a special area, deserving our respect and consideration. Furthermore, I would like to see everyone have positive experiences while there, and by warning beforehand of possible problems, I hope they will be avoided.

I always outline these possibilities to seminar participants, and they are also a part of my *Sedona, Arizona, Energy Vortexes* audio programs. K.D. of Seattle, Washington, must have thought I was being a bit overly concerned, though, and wrote me this humorous, tongue-in-cheek note entitled "Love-on-the-Rocks":

> "Contemplating my first lustless encounter in the vortex, I ruminate on the hazards. Will I worry about what's in my sleeping bag, outside, or both? Should my boots be on or off, and will it be okay not to be pointing north? What if the cheesecloth gets all wadded up and my quartz crystal goes askew from its third-eye position? Will the fact that my car is illegally parked affect performance? Will I be shot by the guard if I return by the wrong fire trail? Will the physical activity be exaggerated if it's the new moon? Is it okay to make love in the desert to a Scorpio born in the year of the Snake, and do I dare to ask, in all sincerity, 'Was it okay for you, too, honey?'"

On the other hand, I was chided by M.P. of Virginia Beach, Virginia, for *not* mentioning a couple of other hazards. Said Monica, "Also, recommend that people bring hiking shoes or boots (cactus goes right through tennis shoes and it's impossible to avoid all of it) and leather gloves (saved my hands and aided in the steep maneuvering)."

MEDITATIONS

Meditating in an energy-enhanced area can be a fulfilling and uplifting experience. In this section, I have included several meditations for you to use at home or in the Sedona vortexes.

Before beginning each meditation, follow the instructions for achieving an altered state of consciousness as described earlier, or use your own favorite technique. At the end of each meditation, count yourself up from one to five and say the words, "wide awake, wide awake."

Below are excerpts from the meditations for your personal use. If you like, you can use the following scripts to make your own recording.

Focusing Healing Vortex Energy Meditation

To listen to this audio meditation, visit www.hayhouse. com/download and enter the Product ID **6829** and Download Code **audio**.

(Begin altered state induction. [See Chapter 7, page 74.])
And I am now completely relaxed and at ease, and I feel total peace surrounding me here in the vortex. And I call out to my own guides and Masters to join me here in this place of intense energy. I seek your assistance. I seek to walk the spiritual path and to expand my awareness. I seek the wisdom to rise above my karma, and I seek healing. I ask for Thy assistance in healing my body and mind. I ask that you combine your energy with the energy of this vortex to heal me now. I am open to healing! And I now draw down the healing light from above and I draw up the intense healing energy of the vortex below. I perceive an iridescent, shimmering, blue light coming down from above and entering

my body. This is the universal life energy . . . the healing energy . . . the God energy . . . and I now feel it filling my body to overflowing with the healing power.

Concentrate now. Totally concentrate upon combining the blue healing light from above, and the intense healing energy of the vortex below . . . I remain totally focused upon increasing and expanding the healing energy. My own guides and Masters assist me in focusing and concentrating and increasing and expanding the healing energy that now pulsates through my body with every beat of my heart.

Concentrate now . . . concentrate . . . concentrate . . . concentrate on the healing light and energy . . . concentrate . . . I keep my mind focused totally upon the healing energy . . .

(Three minutes of silence.)

And the internal healing energy continues to expand and I am now going to begin to focus the energy in the palms of both my hands. I continue to concentrate upon combining the blue healing light from above and the intense energy of the vortex below. At the same time, I direct this intense energy into the palms of both my hands . . . and, as I do, my hands become hotter and hotter . . . and I will continue to focus the energy into my hands until they become so intensely hot that I can hardly stand it any longer . . . I will then place my hands upon the portion of my body with the greatest need for healing.

(Repeat the following for four or five minutes):

And the healing energy concentrates in the palms of my hands and my hands become hotter and hotter . . . hotter and hotter. I am healing . . . I am healed . . . I am healing . . . I am healed.

I once more place my hands upon my body and transfer the intense concentrated energy directly to the area where

it is most needed . . . and I am healing . . . I am healed . . .
I am healing . . . I am healed . . . I am healing . . . I am healed.
(One minute of silence)

And now, for a few moments, I will visualize my body as
perfectly healthy and fully healed.
(Three minutes of silence)

And I have just perceived my own reality. From this
moment on, I experience a physically healthy reality . . . I
am healed.

And from this moment on, I am connected on a superconscious level of mind with this vortex. I can always draw
upon this spiritual healing energy no matter where I am in
the world. The connection is made, and it is complete.

And it is now time to return to the manifest world and
the physical beauty of the vortex. And I thank you, my
guides and Masters, for your assistance, your sharing, and
your love. From this moment on, whenever I feel any form of
negativity, anxiety, or fear, I will sense your gentle presence.
And I will respond to the situation as you would respond—
with love, a tranquil mind, and a compassionate heart.
(Awaken.)

Focusing Vortex Crystal Energy Meditation

(Begin altered state induction. [See Chapter 7, page 74.])
And I am now holding a quartz crystal in my hand . . .
and I am completely relaxed and at ease and I feel total peace
surrounding me here in the vortex. And I'm now going to
take a few moments to concentrate upon the intense energy
that is emitting from the ground beneath me. I feel the

energy . . . I absorb the energy . . . I am physically and mentally charged by the energy.

(One minute of silence)

And I perceive the energy on every level of my body and
mind . . . and I now call out to my own guides and Masters
to join me here in this place of intense energy. I seek your
assistance. I seek to walk the spiritual path and I seek the
wisdom to rise above my karma.

I now choose to combine my own energy with that of
the vortex and with that of my guides and Masters. I now
focus this intense combination of energy into my crystal,
concentrating the energy into the crystal . . . concentrating
the energy into the crystal . . . and I can feel it expanding . . .
pulsating and expanding.

Crystals focus energy and amplify body energy and
thoughts . . . and my crystal also amplifies the energy of the
vortex . . . and it is increasing and expanding . . . charging . . .
and I can now feel the energy pulsation . . . pulsing . . . pulsing
. . . intensifying and building . . . and for a few moments
I will totally concentrate upon the combination of energy
generating within the crystal.

(Two minutes of silence)

And I now quiet my mind and open to the messages that
I shall receive through the vibrations of the crystal. I will
remain in silence, open to insight and guidance. I feel divine
presence . . . I sense the light . . . I feel the love.

(Several minutes of silence)

(Awaken.)

Calling In Vortex Spirits Meditation

To listen to this audio meditation, visit www.hayhouse.com/download and enter the Product ID **6829** and Download Code **audio**.

(Begin altered state induction. [See Chapter 7, page 74.])

And the essence of the energy vortex engulfs me. I feel completely relaxed and at ease . . . surrounded by total peace, balance, and harmony. And I'm now going to take a few moments to concentrate upon the intense energy that is emitting from the ground beneath me. I feel the energy . . . I absorb the energy . . . I am physically and mentally charged by the energy.

(One minute of silence)

And I perceive the energy on every level of my body and mind . . . and I now call out to my own guides and Masters to join me here in this place of intense energy. I seek your assistance. I seek to walk the spiritual path and expand my awareness . . . and I seek the wisdom to rise above my karma. I now choose to combine my own energy with that of the vortex . . . and with that of my guides and Masters, and I seek communication with the spirits of this vortex. I can sense your presence . . . I can feel your intensity . . . and I desire to communicate directly with you at this time.

I will remain in silence . . . open to insight and communication from any positive spirit that remains here in this vortex environment. I await your communication and once I feel it, I will send out my thoughts and questions in the silent language . . . and I will await your response . . . which I will perceive as an internal thought or visual impression.

And I am open now . . . I await you with loving anticipation.

(Several minutes of silence)

And it is now time to return to the manifest world and the physical beauty of this vortex. I thank the spirits of the vortex and I thank my guides and Masters for your assistance, your sharing and love. From this moment on, whenever I feel any form of negativity, anxiety, or fear, I will sense your gentle presence . . . and I will respond to the situation as you would respond, with love and compassion . . . and with a tranquil mind.

(Awaken.)

Testing Unseen Energy Meditation

(Begin altered-state induction. [See Chapter 7, page 74.])

And I am now completely relaxed and at ease and I feel total peace surrounding me here in the vortex. And I call out to my own guides and Masters to join me here in this place of intense energy. I seek your assistance. I seek to walk the spiritual path to expand my awareness . . . and I seek the wisdom to rise above my karma.

My immediate desire is to test the energy of this environment I now find myself within. I now open to all impressions and visualizations . . . and the first and second fingers on my right hand will serve as initial indicators. Through sensory input from my higher mind and my guides and Masters, I will be able to feel answers in my fingers. I will always be able to sense more intense sensations in one finger or the other. If I feel any sensations in my first, or index finger, I am perceiving positive energy . . . or an affirmative yes answer to my inner question. If I feel sensations in my second finger, I am perceiving negative energy . . . or a negative answer to my internal question.

So now to begin . . . I'm going to take a few moments to concentrate upon the intense energy of this environment. I feel the energy . . . I absorb the energy . . . and I now test the energy.

(One minute of silence)

And I now seek to know more about this environment, so I open to visions, impressions, or I may choose to ask subjective questions and perceive the response in my fingers. I ask God and my guides and Masters to be with me now as I explore that which is unseen to me.

(Several minutes of silence)

(Awaken.)

CHAPTER 8

UNUSUAL VORTEX EXPERIENCES WITH AURAS, SOUNDSCAPES, AND DOORWAYS

As I mentioned before, the vortex experiences I am relating in this book represent several years' worth of research and thousands of reports from Sedona Psychic Seminar participants and others who have written regarding their encounters with vortex energy. However, even people who have never heard of the vortexes have also had unusual experiences in Sedona. Sometimes, after they find out about the Sedona vortexes, they write me about what happened to them. Typical of letters I have received from those unfamiliar with Sedona's special energy is the following from J.P. of Studio City, California:

"I am registered for your seminar in Sedona, Arizona. I would like to explain why.

"About five years ago, I was hypnotized and asked to describe a place. I described the Sedona area in detail. I was asked where the place I described was located, but I did not know as I had never seen Sedona before.

"About two and a half years ago, I arrived in Sedona to discover it was the place I had described under hypnosis. I returned to Sedona several times during the next year or so; then, about a year ago, I had two very unusual experiences. The first occurred one day while hiking off the highway to Flagstaff. I was alone as I became very emotional—laughing and crying at the same time for no apparent reason. That went on for approximately 15 minutes as I was coming down the mountain. I didn't understand anything about what had happened, except it seemed to be some type of spiritual experience.

"I returned to Sedona a few weeks later and was driving up the highway toward Flagstaff just outside Sedona when I became very emotional again. That subsided, and I was a bit confused until I realized, as I was later returning to Sedona, that the same things happened as I approached a certain location. Then it dawned on me that it was the same area where I had the intense experience weeks earlier.

"I related these experiences to several friends, and they made statements like 'It must have been the altitude.'

"Then I received the information in the Self-Help Update on Sedona. As I read your article, I could hardly believe the statements made by participants in your seminar. They were so similar to what

I had experienced. The big difference was that I had no knowledge of the vortexes in Sedona!"

These days it is increasingly difficult to find those who have not read or heard about such unusual occurrences. It will therefore be more difficult to ascertain whether the experiences related by those visiting Sedona are affected by things they have previously read or been told about the area. And, in a way, this is what makes the experiences related here even more unique. They have come from people all over the country who attended different seminars and never met or spoke with most of the other people who wrote to us; yet, time after time, we see similar patterns emerging in the experiences related.

Don't be concerned, however, that reading these experiences will affect your imagination or your own experiences. You will know when you experience things in meditation, regression, or self-hypnosis. You will be able to tell if it is real or not. Some of the most powerful regressions I have ever had all seemed as though I were "just making it up," and yet, the information I gained through these experiences was usually accurate and verifiable and always related to my present life. So trust yourself and what you perceive, and you will be able to relate its validity for your own personal situation.

There's nothing wrong with having a little healthy skepticism either. One should approach all spiritual experiences with an open mind. As I warned earlier, spirits can be lower as well as higher vibrations, and it's a good idea to use common sense in evaluating your experiences. Obviously, there are things that happen to us that we can never explain, but as I said, if something real happens to you, you will "know" it.

M.K.W.'s report is an example:

"I made this trip purely for the seminar, not the vortex stuff. Frankly, I didn't believe in it. However, the moment I arrived in Sedona, I felt it. I felt there was bad in the energy as well as good—whatever you brought here (positive or negative) would be enhanced. At the seminar, of course, I heard this as true. I thoroughly enjoyed every aspect of the seminar and feel the block I had been having has been removed. I am now a believer in the vortexes."

AURAS

Another phenomenon that seems to keep recurring in reports from the Sedona vortexes is the appearance of auras or "hazes" in the vortex areas, especially over Bell Rock and Courthouse Rock. Since Bell Rock is supposedly a beacon vortex with energy emitting from the base and extending out the top for miles into the air, it is quite possible that especially sensitive individuals might actually be able to see the energy, or "aura," of the rock. It is also interesting that most claim to see the color of the auras as blue.

"I had a wide range of experiences from seeing the pulsing energy around the Courthouse Rock formation to experiencing a past life in the Boynton Canyon area, viewing the canyon as it was more than two hundred years ago."

R.L.J.
Dallas, Texas

"I went to Airport Mesa for a sunrise meditation. I was winded from the climb and took a few deep breaths, and as I looked out across the valley, I saw the energy emanating from the vortex. It appeared as vertical waves and spirals. It was incredible."

V.W.
Tacoma, Washington

"I saw an iridescent blue-green aura over the hills. I focused and it went away. I unfocused and it returned. Also, the sky pulsated in patches of pale purplish yellow."

F.P.
Detroit, Michigan

"I did get a feeling of the eternal patience of women from Cathedral Rock, and it had a lovely blue aura."

T.G.
Auburn, New Hampshire

"At Bell Rock, about 2 o'clock on a bright, sunny day, I was sitting at a point about halfway to the top. After trying to meditate, I began listening to one of the tapes and my sleepy eyes almost closed. Then, from the background of a nearby bush, I could see a fog or smoke-like substance moving rapidly up the slope. With my eyes fully open, I could see nothing, but returning to a squint, it could be seen again. I thought there must be something here."

J.T.S.
Denver, Colorado

"Sunday at dusk, my friend and I went out to Cathedral Rock. He put me into an altered state, and when I opened my eyes, I saw—with physical vision—one of the most amazing sights I've ever witnessed. The sky was still light enough to make out the clouds that seemed to emanate from the Cathedral Rock structure. Exactly when I opened my eyes, the entire sky was pulsating! It went from darker to lighter with the rhythms of a heartbeat. First the sky was bright, then it was shadowy. The sky and clouds were both affected. I have no doubt that I was witnessing with my physical eyes the energy heartbeat coming from Cathedral Rock. I was blown away!"

**Name Withheld
Burbank, California**

"I went to Boynton Canyon because of the balance. I found a very large flat rock to lie down on. For some strange reason, I could not outline a pentagram, so I used a pyramid, using rocks for each of the corners, and lay down in the middle of it. My message was that I needed the energy and healing powers. After quite a while (I lost track of time), I was told to turn over, so I lay face down. I was told I could take the rocks I was using for the corners to make the pyramid after I returned home whenever my energy got low.

"The next day I went up Bell Rock. Aside from the energy I felt when I was leaning on it, I was delighted to see a beautiful turquoise aura around the top. When I closed my left eye and looked only with my right, the color immediately widened.

"I experienced visions of a beautiful blue crystal under Sedona. I had the feeling of a pyramid lying on its side. I have seen crystals in the window of an optometrist's shop with the same blue crystal."

N.S.

"As my husband and I were leaving, I impulsively asked him to stop at Bell Rock. I took the binoculars to look again at the top. I examined it for perhaps a minute or two and saw nothing unusual. Suddenly, the entire top of the peak was surrounded by a deep purple, pulsing aura. I didn't realize what could be wrong with the glasses, thinking it was some kind of reflection. I've never seen an aura before, but it finally dawned on me that must be what it was. After a while, it disappeared."

A.B.E.

"Airport Mesa: I went there by myself at dusk. I stood by the cliffs, looking at Bell Rock. I 'saw' white energy coming out of Bell Rock, but from its sides, not from the top. On the rocks to the left of Bell Rock, there was a strong blue haze; on the rocks to the right, a white haze. I had to unfocus my eyes to see it, but even so, this is not at all normal for me, and I am sure I would not have seen it in broad daylight."

R.H.W.
Woodland Hills, California

"I initially 'tripped' for half an hour, which did relax me enough so that I was able to concentrate. As I opened my eyes while in my reclining position, I literally saw a dark blue light emanating from the sky, entering my head and my upturned palms. This is not my normal psychic modus operandi. I am very intuitive, but my visualizations have always been sketchy fragments against the darkness of my closed eyes. Still skeptical that this was only an optical adjustment to the bright sky, I moved my palms toward my body, then away from it. The light followed! My connection with God has always been strong, and His effect on my life profound, but this was more than I had ever expected from the vortex."

A.L.

SOUND

Bell Rock Vortex also seems to have another unusual quality—that of sound. Several individuals have reported hearing everything from bell tones and rumblings to beeps in the vicinity of the rock.

"At Bell Rock, my companion and I heard a very high-pitched, sharp, bell-like sound. It was clear and beautiful."

E.G.
Alameda, California

"At the Bell Rock Vortex, there was this sound, similar to thunder or a sonic boom, but it came from the Bell Rock, not the sky. I'm not sure what it was, but for me, it was very interesting to stand on Bell Rock, listening to this rumbling thunder that seemed to emanate from within the rock."

Name Withheld
Long Beach, California

"Bell Rock Vortex seemed to call to me in an inaudible voice. I felt the energy from the highway as we were driving. Once we began climbing upon the rocks, I could feel their vibrations and could hear the rocks humming. I also felt a 'Star' or 'Interplanetary Connection' in this vortex."

P.A.
Council Bluffs, Iowa

"I went to Bell Rock at dawn and planned to do my Tai Chi Chuan exercise with the sunrise. I had only done a few movements when I slowly collapsed to the ground. My legs gave out under me and I could barely move.

"I also heard a beeping sound from the mountain next to Bell Rock and then the same sound came from the top of Bell Rock. This beeping occurred about six times totally. I was told through automatic writing that the formation next to Bell Rock was hollow. I was also told that the reason I collapsed was because my body is unaccustomed to such energy and I 'short-circuited' as one would say."

D.K.
Aptos, California

Some have suggested that because this vortex is supposed to attract UFOs, perhaps the sounds are in some way related. In fact, one seminar participant, an engineer who requested we only use his initials, said his wife actually claimed to see UFOs above Bell Rock. Although he wasn't able to see any UFOs himself, one of the photos he took at the time showed a strange spherical object above Bell Rock. The film lab could find no explanation for it. Here is his description of the encounter.

"Besides being the best organized and best run seminar [that] my wife and I ever attended, it was the best preparation we could think of to experience Sedona and the vortex energies. For the six days that we were in

Sedona, we experienced nonstop, round-the-clock psychic phenomena, each one better than the other. The experience I would like to relate is the physical manifestation of a UFO on film that we could not see physically but appeared on a slide after it was developed.

"After arriving in Sedona and participating in the seminar, my wife and I noticed that we became extremely aware and sensitive to energies. We were attracted to the Bell Rock Vortex because of its known association with UFO sightings. My wife could see ships in the etheric [sic] above Bell Rock. I was frustrated because I couldn't see them, but had a feeling that if I took several photos of Bell Rock, maybe something might just turn up on the film. Besides, I am an engineer by profession and have always wanted physical proof I could show someone and verify concerning the 'paranormal.'

"Upon developing the 180 slides I took on the trip, one slide had a purple spherical 'object' on it, directly above Bell Rock. There were no spots on any of the other slides. Some may say it's just a coincidence. The film lab confirmed that it was not a chemical spot on the slide. I know what it is!"

J.S.

THE DOORWAY

I never cease to be fascinated by the similarities that appear in the reports on the vortexes. One particularly interesting situation involved four participants who claimed to see a doorway. Three of them were in the vortex at the same time but in different areas; the fourth was at another seminar. Here are three of their stories:

"Meditating at the left base of Bell Rock, my attention focused on the mountain to the right, just above the horizon, where I observed a small, bell-shaped peak protrusion. At this spot, there appeared to be a doorway extending to the top of the universe.

"I was impressed: 'All is possible in the positive vortex energy. All one need do is find the spot and one can then enter the doorway, which is open to all; all who enter will go to the outer world and will be given eternal life.'

"After a while, I was instructed to bring a rock to my friend, Emma. Later, when I met her, I learned that she and another party had discovered a doorway just above the horizon of the mountain to the left of Bell Rock. I gave her the rock as instructed, whereupon she noticed [that] its shape [was] the same as the doorway she and the other party had seen."

M.P.G.
Oakland, California

"At Bell Rock, I heard one high-pitched, sharp bell-like sound, very clear and beautiful. Turning to the west, I visualized the vortex energy taking shape as a doorway. Margaret Glatt shared the above experiences with me and a man named Tony also saw the doorway."

E.G.
Alameda, California

"Spirits guided a friend and me to our special spot. He wanted to be near a riverbed, but I wanted to be near the pine trees. We found a spot where the riverbed ran over a large bed of rocks, like a short waterfall, by three pine trees. I did fantastic automatic writing and meditated.

"Upon finishing my meditation, I was guided to look up and there I saw a spirit on the mountain looking over us. He came through a doorway and looked at me. I felt an intense surge of energy. I came unglued at this sight, wondering whether I were really here or in a dream."

J.M.

CHAPTER 9

VORTEX ENERGY EXPERIENCES

One thing everyone who visits Sedona agrees on is the tremendous energy of the area and the extraordinary effects it has on people. Many report feelings of euphoria or contentment, and a common result is that most seem to need less sleep, food, and liquids during their stay. Increased physical stamina was another experience, and some even found that the energy sometimes seemed to transfer into inanimate objects, especially metallic ones. Those who live in Sedona eventually seem to attune to the energy so that they are able to "normalize" their behavior.

These are just some of the many reactions to the energy of Sedona and the vortex areas.

"My most interesting vortex experience was simply the incredible energy I felt, especially from Bell Rock. It was such a natural high! The whole area induces euphoria; you feel as though you don't have a care in the world! We returned again to Boynton Canyon and Bell

Rock on Monday. They are such addicting places—we feel an increasingly strong attraction to the vortexes. I'm in California right now, but I just want to be meditating in Boynton Canyon. It is such a letdown to be away from Sedona. I've never felt so drawn or seduced by an area."

J.L.M.

"I have never hiked in my life and after 12 miles felt like I'd walked a city block! The Airport Mesa Vortex is the only one that didn't faze me at all. The other two were about as strong as the islands of Kauai, Maui, and Kona in Hawaii."

E.G.
Alameda, California

"Boynton Canyon had an energy that could be seen by staring past the rock formations, best described as an intermittent spectrum arcing. I called down the white light, and bam! the white light hit. A powerful wind rocked my body, my hair flapped across my face, and as I accepted the safe, all-protective light, the wind softened and slowly stopped. I usually get colors that I can view within the whole front of my forehead, but never blue. This grey-blue was powerful. Twenty minutes later, more white light and the powerful wind sequence and more wonderful blue light."

C.Y.
Vista, California

"The energy level we experienced was unbelievable! After almost two hours of walking and exploring at high altitude, I felt no stress or strain. I averaged four hours of sleep a night and did not feel like I needed any more."

R.L.J.
Dallas, Texas

"My experiences at the vortexes were incredible. Getting to the vortex was a physical struggle for me. But in the Medicine Wheel at the Airport Mesa Vortex, the energy was the most electrifying physical experience I can remember having. I felt the old energy being drawn from my total self, replaced by a renewed, revitalized supply of energy that consumed my entire being. I literally felt shooting electric charges coming into my body that held me completely spellbound for several minutes. The change in my physical self was so exhilarating that I suddenly felt as if I were a young girl again with boundless energy and a carefree spirit.

"We left to go to Boynton Canyon, where I found myself climbing the canyon ridges alongside young girls in their twenties, just as if I had never had a physical impairment nor any fear of heights. Let me point out that not only was I physically unable to exert myself in this way, but that I was also extremely afraid of heights. Yet we walked for miles and climbed for hours that afternoon, and I couldn't remember how long it had been since I felt such renewed energy and positive mental attitude.

"Since returning home, my daily existence is filled with greater peace. I have a deep knowing that I am connected to the energy of the universe. I allow that energy to guide me on a daily basis, leading to new frontiers."

S.L.W.
Kansas City, Missouri

"At Airport Mesa, I chose a spot on a ledge to meditate, holding my favorite crystals in each hand. I then surrounded myself with white light, but it appeared different than before, having many sparks of silver energy. I asked for assistance from my guides and medicine animals, and immediately felt a very strong energy from my crystals. I felt a tremendous tingling and warmth in my hands. It was much stronger than anything I've ever experienced. I began to cry, I felt so good."

E.K.
Torrance, California

"We find Sedona energetic and invigorating. We felt this on our very first trip to Arizona in 1978. We bought property at that time—Village of Oak Creek. We both feel more psychic here than we normally are."

A.R.T.
Phoenix, Arizona

"The amount of energy I was able to absorb in Sedona —particularly in Boynton Canyon—was absolutely amazing! I was able to get by on four hours of sleep. While at home I usually need ten hours, and even then, still wake up tired. I had more energy there in Sedona than I've ever had in my life. This energy lasted about three days after I left Sedona; each day the energy was a little less than the day before until I became the same tired old rag I had been before the trip. A person could really get hooked on a high like that."

Name Withheld
Palmdale, California

"My experience at Airport Mesa was literally electrifying! I had been asked by various friends to take their crystals with me to charge with vortex energy. By the time I got to my own—the largest—even with my eyes closed, I could see a clear blue-white light, so bright it was almost painful. The energy was surging through my body into the crystals. It was like being a human jumper cable to the cosmos."

G.E.K.
Wichita, Kansas

"On the first day, we went to Bell Rock. I weigh 320 pounds, so we didn't go very far 'up' to meditate (three steps up produced heavy breathing, legs trembling, sweat pouring off me, etc.).

"On the last day, we went back. It was strange— neither my wife nor I felt the least bit tired. I walked and climbed as though I were 18 again, instead of 46. We made it at least halfway up Bell Rock to the huge ledge that runs around the middle. My legs felt very young and springy, and I experienced no out-of- breath panting, no perspiration. My wife and I both talked about it wonderingly."

R.K.P.
Oxnard, California

"At around 5 o'clock, I went to Bell Rock. When I got there, the feeling of relief was fantastic. My whole body was tingling with energy. Once I got out of my car and started walking, I couldn't stop. I felt as though 20 years had dropped off my 40-year-old frame, and I just kept going with no feeling of fatigue at all.

"I couldn't get over the beauty of the area. It was as though I had been there before and I had finally got- ten back, and it was just sooo great to be home!"

J.C.H.
Lynn, Massachusetts

"My wife and I went to the Airport Mesa Vortex. After the sun went down, it got chilly and the chill brought me out of an altered state. When I arose and began to write, my wedding ring immediately attracted my attention. It's gold with five diamonds, the center diamond being the largest. The ring was glowing, glaringly! I have never cleaned it, though I had thought to do so about a week before the seminar. When my wife came out of her trance state, I said nothing to her about the ring, waiting to see if she would notice it too. And, although by now it was not as bright as it was when I first awakened, she noticed the glow immediately. She said that you couldn't miss it! It was really extremely bright, and now the ring has enlarged itself!

"One more thing that is beyond our ability to understand: We're from Gresham, Oregon, and drove down in our '83 Honda Accord. Somehow, our car became electrified while in Sedona; the longer we stayed, the more charged up it became. By the time we left Sedona, the car was shocking us up to a distance of four inches away. The power lessened the farther we drove from Sedona. I'm glad, because we were really getting tired of being electrocuted."

J.M.M.
Gresham, Oregon

"After the vortex experience, my life is totally changing. I knew it would as I was leaving, and I've found that my outer and inner vision are both much improved. My eyes were totally clear and sparkling when I arrived home Tuesday night after driving straight through for 13 hours. Also, I brought home a couple of small pebbles from the Airport Mesa Vortex and put them in a plant that was almost dead. It is now healthy, green, happy, and blooming.

"I brought another small stone to a friend, who immediately experienced benefits from it. She had been feeling tired and down when I gave it to her, but after an hour of holding the stone, she looked and felt totally different."

D.C.

"The few small stones I brought home with me from the vortex have a definite magnetic field around them. Several people have reported this. I know that, as agreed, I will have to return these stones to the place from which I took them. I tried laying them on my chakra centers this morning, and the 'boost' was powerful and most helpful. A professional psychic came within 20 feet of me and claimed to feel 'tremendous energy' coming from my body. She asked if she could hug me and afterward thanked me for it. She did not know where I had been at that time (later I told her)."

I.S.
Corona, California

"From the moment we entered the vortex area, I felt an inexplicable euphoria overtake me. The feeling was akin to having consumed a few drinks without the negative effects of alcohol. After three hours of sleep, I had no trouble at all completing the 10-hour drive to my California home."

Name Withheld
Burbank, California

"I went to Boynton Canyon with several other girls I met at the seminar. I'm not very physically active and had noticed the high altitude of Sedona was causing me to be short of breath. In addition, I was carrying a 25-pound backpack as I walked the rather steep incline of Boynton Canyon. I felt sure I would be totally exhausted upon reaching a place to meditate but, instead, found myself so energized that I had difficulty reaching an alpha level."

M.L.A.
Clearwater, Florida

"In visiting the Boynton Canyon area, Bell Rock, and Courthouse [Rock], I experienced the feeling of energy, but nothing else. I was on a constant energy high the whole time I was in Sedona. I also seemed to require less sleep but when I did, I continually had dreams I had dreamed when I was younger (approximately 5 to 15 years of age)."

J.D.
Calistoga, California

"The vortex experience was awesome! I was feeling depressed and extremely tired as I drove to Boynton Canyon. As I neared the area, I suddenly felt euphoric and so full of energy [that] I climbed nearly to the top of the main mountain in Boynton Canyon. I've felt utter peace and joy ever since! I feel totally in control of my own life now—confident, full of joy, and completely energized! I'm very fortunate to live so close, so I'll visit the area every month if I can."

F.M.
Phoenix, Arizona

CHAPTER 10

HEALING VORTEX EXPERIENCES

The vortex experience easiest for people to accept is physical healing. You have a pain, a wound, or abnormal condition, and it disappears. If medical tests concur with the manifestation of a cure, it moves the healing experience out of the realm of the imagination and into the world of accepted reality. Physical healings seem to be a common occurrence among visitors to the vortexes according to the reports we have on file.

One particularly interesting case was that of N.H. of Mesa, Arizona. She experienced a healing at her first Sedona Psychic Seminar. Then, about a year later, she had another surprise. These are the two reports we received from her, in the order delivered:

"It was the first time I had ever been in a prayer circle. When you said to ask for self-healing . . . I put in my feet. I had a slight growth problem on the sides of each foot. Of course, after the circle ended, I checked out my feet. They were still the same and I thought, *Oh, well, it was worth a shot*. Then, about four weeks later, I had my feet propped up on the coffee table and noticed something different about them. I examined them and was totally amazed—my feet were normal! There was and is no growth problem, and I have very proudly worn sandals the rest of the summer.

"Nine years ago, the doctors told me I was sterile. I was divorced and had two sons [at home] at the time, so I wasn't upset. . . . I went through the healing circle in Sedona, and six months later in Scottsdale. The Sedona Healing Circle really did a beautiful job of healing my feet; I never dreamed [I] would also [become] pregnant.

"[T]he doctor did a sonogram test . . . I was amazed to watch my baby moving into his brother. Yes, I'm having twins. Thank God I didn't go through three healing circles!"

The following are the words of others who have received healing in the vortexes.

"Five doctors had advised me that the stress of several vexing personal problems was literally killing me. I went to the Sedona Psychic Seminar to try to rid myself of the results of stress, [and] then recharge myself and my life with energy from the vortex. Many great things did occur, but only after the healing circle. Bell Rock sent me soaring in meditation and I received the 'breakthrough' I went to Sedona for. Since then, I am experiencing great things of all sorts almost daily. My health is vastly improved and I feel great. People say I look years younger."

L.S.
Perryton, Texas

"The two guides who had appeared to me on the black screen in the clairvoyant session the night before, appeared not as a vision, but in voice only. They identified themselves when I went to the vortex. I wasn't expecting a lot, but I knew I'd receive all that I had come for at this time. I was instructed to walk along a dry wash, which I did, until I felt I was in the right place. This was a huge rock, which was shaped like the palm of the left hand. I stood on the rock and raised my arms upward and immediately felt a warm, vibrating feeling on my hands. I was told, 'Heal thyself,' and was instructed to squeeze the poisons from the back of my leg above the knee, where I have a lump about the size of a cherry tomato. I was then led to walk in the wash.

"As my body was being filled with energy, the feeling of being very light-headed gradually disappeared and I knew when my body was 'back in balance.' When I left the vortex, all that was left was a small lump about as big as the tip of my smallest finger, and by Sunday, it was gone entirely."

A.R.W.

"I received healing for the torn muscles in my back when I went to Bell Rock. I had torn the muscles in my back two weeks prior to the seminar. I knew I couldn't do any climbing but felt I would receive at least some benefits. I sat with my back against the rock base for quite a long time facing the sun. I felt warmed clear through.

"When I rose to leave, I looked back at Bell Rock and saw a very old man (I felt he was the high priest of all the high priests) suspended in front of Bell Rock. He didn't say anything; he just looked at me. He was dressed in a greyish-white robe, and I felt I knew him. I felt he was trying to help me remember. Later, in the seminar, we did a regression, and during this, I experienced more about the priest."

M.P.
Escondido, California

"Bell Rock Vortex . . . was a healing point for me. Both times, my hands became extremely hot and I asked for healing powers to intensify, and it seems they have. Airport Mesa last year was too intense for me. I could not handle it physically. However, this year, it was very different, although I felt like I was falling over forward. Boynton Canyon was freeing, calming, and very soothing."

S.H.
Lompoc, California

"My mom, who has had spinal arthritis all her life, has been in a lot of pain lately. She's had to walk with a cane and hasn't been doing very much. Well, from the circle I sent her the healing power as . . . directed. She reports that she hasn't been using the cane since Sunday evening (the time we did the healing circle). She also says she's feeling better than she has in years."

H.C.F.
Alhambra, California

"We visited the Boynton Canyon Vortex Sunday afternoon after the final session of the seminar. We played the Crystal Cave tape along with one of your vortex tapes. During deep meditation, two of us were aware of the visitation of Indian spirits, seeming to look us over and giving their approval.

"I was shown a portion of the cells of my body—the 'space' areas were shining with white light. I felt as if I had experienced purification and healing of my entire body."

Name Withheld
Fresno, California

In an article titled "Healing Power of Sedona" that ran in Issue 43 of my *Master of Life* magazine, Sharon Boyd explored the healing experiences of Sedona Psychic Seminar participants.

Sedona—the name conjures up images of magic and mystery. Thousands of metaphysically oriented people have come to Sedona to attend Dick Sutphen's Psychic Seminars, and have experienced exciting enhancements of their latent psychic abilities.

The sense of peace and serenity, the enhancement of psychic abilities, the easy camaraderie of like-minded people, and the sheer beauty of the surrounding countryside are some of the reasons people respond to the pull of Sedona.

In previous issues, we have focused on the psychic manifestations almost everyone experiences in the seminar. The following accounts are tales of the healing powers of the vortexes that participants have eagerly related—healings both incredible and trivial, as the gift of the spirits of the vortexes or resulting from the realignment of energy restoring the harmonious balance within the body.

Edgar Cayce viewed balanced body energies as crucial to good health: "The human body is made up of electronic vibration, with each atom and element of the body, each organ and organism of same, having the electronic vibration necessary for the sustenance of and equilibrium in that particular organism."

Recent findings have repeatedly affirmed the link between mind and health. And in the last decade or two, there has been a large-scale turning away from traditional, symptom-oriented medicine toward preventive and holistic medicine with its emphasis on healing as an innate, latent capacity of the integrated mind-body, waiting to be released or unblocked.

"Two years ago today, I arrived in Sedona just a few short days before the Sedona Psychic Seminar. I came for a number of reasons. Having had five throat operations, with a promise of more to come, I needed a healing. I was desperate! My marriage was also in the process of breaking up. I had no support in my beliefs whatsoever and I longed for a new start.

"Indeed, I became like new! A healing on my throat took place in Boynton Canyon. In meditation, I was led to an Indian spirit of Boynton Canyon. Upon asking for a healing, I made a vow to work for Mother Earth in exchange. I was so grateful, yet knew nothing of Earth work at the time.

"At the Airport Mesa Vortex, I sat in the car of a friend of mine. We watched the view of Sedona at night. The energy was unusually high. I felt strange, as if something were waiting for the right moment to take over. Reaching out, I took my friend's hand. The moment I touched it, we both felt a huge jolt of energy go through us, like an electric shock. I immediately felt rearranged, as if my cellular structure had completely changed. It was one of many turning points I reached throughout that week.

"My psychic abilities turned out to be greater than I could have ever imagined. And what the participants at the seminar shared was precious—the love, the understanding, and the support—and gave me a new perspective on life!

"During the first week back in Seattle, my co-workers teased me about changing so drastically. My attitude changed, my appearance . . . my whole being shined with a new light. I began to write poems that were published in the local Northwest metaphysical paper. It felt good to have a sense of expression without fearing what others would think.

"My love for Mother Earth grew intensely by the time the Harmonic Convergence came that summer. I wrote more and more articles about our relationships to Mother Earth and to each other. And by November, I found a woman who taught me shamanism. Now it is a way of life for me; I would live no other way.

"Devoted to my vow in Sedona to work for the Earth, I pushed on in my growth. I learned Chi Kung and "light working," and had therapy through massage/ Chi energy often enough to accelerate the process of my ever-changing DNA. I became a shamanic healer with wonderful, absolutely profound outcomes! I took my knowledge to the Seattle Public School District and taught a workshop on shamanic mask-making to a class of junior high school students. I also chaired a nationwide art competition at the same school.

"The time of harvest has come to me now, just two years after Sedona. I am now lecturing and assisting the very people who taught me. I am an ordained Earth Steward and Spiritual Healer and the Seattle representative working voluntarily through Jose Arguelles and Earth Celebration 2000. I've been writing articles for a variety of publications throughout the nation. I am currently working on an article for *Vogue* magazine. I also plan on doing an environmental education program for the Seattle Public School District in the coming year . . . not counting my full-time job and housework!

"I received a clean bill of health on my throat. I never needed surgery again! And my marriage was saved—my husband is my greatest support, lover, and best friend.

"I needed to share this with you on this two-year anniversary of the threefold healing I received in Sedona: physical, emotional, and spiritual."

C.C.
Seattle, Washington

"I first began to realize something was different just outside of Gallup, New Mexico, driving west on Interstate 40 toward Sedona. My face felt flushed. I was wearing an orlon sweater. The temperature outside the car was in the 50s. The vents in the car were open. I was just about to pull my sweater off when I noticed that I was cool, almost chilly, in the car. So I left the sweater on. But then I was too warm.

"As we crept closer and closer to Sedona, my head and upper body alternated between hot flashes and cold sweeping chills although I was perfectly healthy and did not possess even the slightest hint of a cold or anything else. Upon arriving in Sedona, the hot flashes and chills settled simply into my feeling too warm.

"When we arrived at the Airport Mesa Vortex, I felt like I was on fire although the weather was even colder because heavy rain and snow clouds were blanketing the sun. I wanted to meditate in the vortex for just 10 minutes so that I could draw some of the energy there into my body to take with me, but we were unable to find a place without wind or people. [M]y fiancée suggested that we face the vortex and extend the palms of our hands out toward the vortex, so we did. I felt a numbing sensation in my hands. They began to burn. The flame crawled up the internal parts of my arms and consumed my entire body. I was blazing.

"Throughout the rest of that day and the subsequent three days, my mind and body were high on this electromagnetic energy that had permeated me. I was aflame intuitively, intellectually, sexually, and physically. My overall energy was smooth, consuming, and massive.

"At the end of the fourth day, I concluded that I began feeling the powerful energy of the vortexes in Sedona while still on Interstate 40 outside of Gallup, New Mexico. I did not experience any burnout. It has been several days now since we left Sedona. My mind and body have been calm, quiet, and very productive— almost as if they have received tune-ups.

"Remarkably, a stress-induced lower back ailment causing severe muscle spasms and great pain that I have experienced since January of this year is no longer bothering me. I am able to bend over stiff legged and touch my toes without pain for the first time in months. And perhaps even more remarkably, I gave no thought to my back problems when I was in Sedona. The muscles in my lower back, which had felt like a doubled-up fist ever since the spasms, disappeared almost as if on cue after we drove into the city limits of Sedona that first night."

D.V.
Aurora, Colorado

"My sister, my niece, a friend, and I attended the seminar in Sedona in April. Sedona is so beautiful, and the seminar was great! I had super results with the various psychic things we practiced.

"We made it to three of the four vortexes. Bell Rock did the oddest thing for me. I proved it the next day at Airport Mesa.

"The day we went to Bell Rock, I scampered up like a mountain goat and even helped my sister up parts of it. I went out on a tiny ledge with my back to the rock and my feet on the edge of the drop off and meditated there. When finished, I scampered down, once more as nimble, agile, and sure-footed as a mountain goat.

"Dick, I'm 60 years old and have a back problem. Also, for the last 10 years, maybe longer, I have been afraid of heights—not terrified, just terribly unhappy about looking down from a ladder or a roof or over the edge of the Grand Canyon unless I am firmly anchored.

"That's all gone! I don't know why the fear of heights started 10 years ago or why it left me at Bell Rock. Believe me, I'm very happy about that as well as the experiences during meditation there and at the other two vortexes. It will surely make my work around my home easier: painting trim, fixing the roof, cleaning the chimney—all things my 71-year-old brother-in-law has had to help me with before the Sedona seminar are all things I can do for myself now."

E.H.
Forestville, New York

"I am a very active 29-year-old woman. Although I take really good care of myself, I have bad knees. I injured them several years ago; they healed, but I have had chronic arthritic symptoms ever since. Too much physical stress; sudden weather changes; cold, damp, or wet weather make them hurt a lot. Being active, that really hampers my lifestyle.

"My knees were hurting a lot when I left Oregon for Arizona. I tried to put the ache out of my mind while at the seminar sessions on Friday and Saturday. But I have to tell you that I missed the Sunday session and the healing circle because I spent the day at Bell Rock. While having totally healthy knees is always in the back of my mind, I didn't consciously spend my time in the vortexes seeking healing.

"After the seminar, I spent a day in Las Vegas where the temperature was in the 90s. Then I flew back to 60-degree rainy weather in Portland. Since returning home, the weather has been typically foggy, wet, and cold. My knees should have been crying out in agony. But, after being home for a week, it dawned on me that they didn't hurt at all! And they haven't hurt since that Sunday in Sedona. It's been over a month and they still don't hurt. I've been working out daily and karate training three nights a week and still no pain. Temporary or permanent, this is a miracle. I'm loving every minute of it."

K.V.
Corvallis, Oregon

"I experienced a strange and wonderful happening while climbing Bell Rock in Sedona a couple of years ago and I am happy to share it.

"The following explains my mental and physical state at that time. I had just broken up with a man I'd been dating for four years and was brokenhearted. Financially, I was in a very bad situation—broke and between jobs. I had no desire to be alive. I started drinking heavily on the weekends to blot out reality. By September, I came down with bronchitis, a nasty case that took me seven months to shake.

"I went to Sedona and climbed Bell Rock for the first time. I was tired of my hopeless state and was looking for any solution to turn my attitude around. The bronchitis was so bad that I couldn't go more than a few steps before stopping to catch my breath. I came upon a medicine wheel and carefully positioned myself in the middle of it. Looking at the sky, I yielded to a sudden impulse that swept through me and said aloud, 'Please heal me.' Then I started crying.

"The very moment I finished those words, I felt a vibration start from the soles of my feet and slowly surge through my body and out the top of my head. I put my hand above my head once and could feel the force, hot and pulsing, so strong that it pushed my hand away. When the vibration finally left me, I was very excited because I thought any minute my lungs would be clear and I would be able to breathe freely. Wrong!

"The next day, I went to the grocery store. I was out of beer—God forbid. So I went over toward the liquor section. But without even realizing what happened, I walked past the beer and ended up on the other side of the store, picking out vegetables and fruits. I remember grabbing a bunch of bananas and laughing out loud. I thought to myself, *You forgot the beer*. Well, as I once more walked toward the liquor section, I realized that I would never drink again. I knew then what type of healing had taken place the day before.

"That has been over a year ago and I have not had the desire to drink nor even thought about drinking alcohol since. This would not be an earth-shattering story, except that alcoholism runs in my family—my parents are recovered alcoholics and my older brother has been on and off the wagon his entire adult life. So I had resigned myself to the fact that it would take a superhuman effort to cut down or stop drinking, and I always had that little thought in the back of my head that maybe I wouldn't ever be able to stop drinking.

"Oh, the bronchitis healed—a healthy body usually seems to mend itself. But the brokenhearted spirit inside me that had succumbed to the denial of life by self-medicating with alcohol—that's what needed healing. I've made several trips back to Bell Rock to meditate, give thanks, and ask for another miracle. Of course, I do not specify what miracle, just another one, please."

C.M.
Phoenix, Arizona

"I went to Sedona as a cleansing experience, for a new beginning, as did many others, apparently.

"At the Airport Mesa Vortex, I felt very nauseous and threw up. I felt this was my body's way of physically emptying and purifying itself as my mind was doing.

"Sunday morning, I awoke with the stirrings of a migraine headache. I attended the morning session, and then went to lunch. Upon my return, I felt much worse and decided to lie down in the back of my rental car. Of course, I was quite upset at missing the last session, but I was worried about how I would be able to drive unless I did something to alleviate the headache. I laid on the seat, attempting to relax and meditate, to no avail. I knew the healing circle would be held that afternoon and thought I would be able to be rid of my migraine if I could only attend, but I was too ill to get out of the car.

"Later, someone knocked on my car window and advised me that the seminar was over. I opened the door and got out of the car, suddenly feeling fine. The man who knocked on the car window had known of my headache; perhaps his thoughts transferred from the healing circle to me for my healing.

"There is something else that is more exciting to me. I have suffered from poor circulation for years and have always felt cold. But since returning home from Sedona, I have felt very warm, almost tingly—a very comforting feeling. I plan to have my hypoactive thyroid tested to see whether it is now functioning normally."

G.S.
Punxsutawney, Pennsylvania

"Four of us attending the Sedona seminar went to Airport Mesa. I drove, using the vortex location sheet we received in the seminar for directions. I couldn't read the sheet without my glasses, so I made numerous stops to verify our location.

"When we left, one of the girls mentioned that she could see better and farther. We all seemed to [be] having this same experience. To my surprise, I could now read the directions without my glasses.

"I have worn glasses since I was 41. I am now 57. When I got back to the motel, I decided to see if I could read without my glasses. I could."

A.M.M.
Jackson, Michigan

"I just had to write and thank you for the wonderful weekend we spent in Sedona at your seminar this past March. My husband has been interested in psychic stuff for a few years and had ordered the Sedona video and the Sedona book. I wasn't that interested in the psychic stuff, but I did like your self-help and motivational tapes, and had used some of them with good results.

"I have been diagnosed as having systemic lupus. When I saw the Sedona tape my husband sent for, especially when I saw all those people saying how much better they felt after going to the vortexes, I knew I had to go there, even if it was for a psychic seminar I wasn't really interested in. So we made our plans, jumped in the van, and headed for Arizona. I didn't pack much but I didn't care; I just couldn't wait to get there. We arrived the day before the seminar and went to Boynton Canyon. I didn't expect much, but I felt so calm and peaceful, I knew there was something there that I hadn't expected.

"Normally, I cannot walk up hills or too many stairs without experiencing a lot of pain. I climbed as high as I dared; the higher I went, the better I felt. I thought for sure the next day I would be unable to get out of bed.

"But, surprised, I was up early the next day and found myself full of energy and bouncing around. We went to the seminar, and I found myself getting right into that 'psychic stuff.' By Sunday, I was so full of energy that I thought I would burst. The love, the great feeling, and many new friends—I felt as though I had found the pot of gold at the end of the rainbow. It was like getting a double shot of cortisone. I didn't want to leave."

W.P.
Painted Post, New York

"On the last day of the seminar, Easter Sunday, we did psychometry readings with partners. The woman who did a reading for me came up with some very accurate information on me, including a request from my guides to meet them at Bell Rock.

"Bell Rock was the only vortex I had not visited the previous day. I was very excited since my previous efforts to contact my guides had left me feeling vague and doubtful. I felt the need to get to Bell Rock as soon as possible since I was leaving that day.

"It was raining pretty steadily, so I put on some rain gear and walked up the mountain. I stopped at a place near a small waterfall, then found a small place to begin my meditation. Making contact with my guides, I received some interesting and very valuable information about my children. At the end of the meditation, my guides informed me, 'We will tell you more about your healing later. That is all.' Then, a while later, as I was preparing to leave the vortex, they told me my eyes would be healed.

"I have what is considered an incurable disease in my eyes called [ocular] histoplasmosis. It makes the blood vessels in my eyes break and causes scar tissue to form. This scar tissue had formed in the macula in my eye, and I only had peripheral vision in that eye. The macula is the part of the eye where the image focuses; because of the scar tissue, I could not focus that eye on anything. Now I am beginning to see with that eye. All my doctor can tell me is that the scar tissue has thinned somehow and light is being let through.

"I believe my healing has begun and I will have my eyesight back totally. What I experienced that weekend at the seminar was simply the most incredible experience of my life. When my plane took off from the Sedona airport, I felt as though I were leaving home. Sedona is a place I will go back to—I feel I have unfinished business there."

N.H.
Moorhead, Minnesota

Perfection and balance are traditional attributes of spirituality that also underlie the concept of health. Sickness and health are not simply physical states that the modern miracles of science will be able to analyze and make easily understandable. They are rooted in the deepest essence of being.

Science and intellect can show us those aspects of physical reality that can be touched but they cannot probe the deepest mysteries.

You cannot restore health in yourself or in others until you are aware, in the depths of your spirit, what health is. Health is wholeness in its most profound sense. And it is this essential wholeness, this dynamic and harmonious balance, that the healing power of Sedona appears to have restored to the participants whose stories we have shared.

CHAPTER 11

PAST-LIFE REGRESSIONS

As with all other types of psychic energy experiments, exploring past lives through hypnotic regression seems to be enhanced by the energy of the vortexes. Many reported experiences similar to those of C.B.:

> "I was able to see vivid pictures for the very first time. The experience was very exciting, yet frustrating, because putting it into words somehow isn't easy. It comes out so trite-sounding compared to the emotion involved. Also, in the regression experience, I saw things there is no way to explain. I've seen nothing in the world that compares to it."

Here are a few of the past-life regressions encountered during the seminar sessions or in vortex meditations.

"During the past-life regression, I discovered the answer to a dream I had four years ago where I went through a death experience. The same death experience was in the past-life regression.

"In the regression, I was a young [American] Indian girl in the Arizona territory in the 1870s, although I'm not sure it was called Arizona at that time. My tribe was quite small, and we were more or less farmers or cultivators, growing our own foods and medicinal herbs. We were very peaceful people, being more spiritual or metaphysical. I was apprenticed to a very old medicine man, training to become a medicine person.

"An older woman in the village was very jealous of me because the young man I was married to was the one she had wanted her daughter to marry. Also, she wanted her son to become the new medicine man, feeling it would give her greater power in the tribe as she was not well accepted by the others because of her evil ways.

"I remember being adept at many things under the medicine man's guidance, including astral projection. During one such projection, I was shown how to use 'star rocks' quartz crystals as one method of healing. Also, during this time, I was aware that this older woman was plotting my death, but I could do little to prevent it.

"When I was about 19, my husband was killed in a raid on our village by a war party from a neighboring tribe. Later that year, our tribe prepared to move to our winter hunting grounds. I was standing near where the horses were tied when I saw the older woman coming toward me. She was very angry and full of hate. As she approached me, she picked up a long lance and stabbed me through the solar plexus area.

"As I lay dying, I left my body and looked down upon the scene. She was standing over my body, laughing. I saw the rest of the people riding away from our camp. I felt very sad because I felt I could have done so much for my people if I had not died.

"Then a glowing figure came and hovered beside me. I remember calling him the 'being of light.' He told me that this particular life had ended and I must go on to finish my purpose of healing elsewhere.

"My husband in that life is my youngest son in this life; my father in that life was also my father in this life; the woman who killed me is my ex-husband's present wife, bearing the same feelings of malice and hate for me.

"As a child in this life, I have felt fear and uneasiness around [American] Indian people that I could not explain. Also, my father had a great yearning to move to Phoenix—that was all he ever talked about—but we couldn't afford to move from Montana to Arizona at that time. I have also felt this urgency to move to Arizona for about a year and a half.

"I have been told by several psychics that I have been a healer in Atlantis, Lemuria, China, and Egypt, and several times I have been [a] medicine person in the Arizona area. I assume that explains my 'Arizona connection' and my inner feeling that I should move there."

P.A.
Council Bluffs, Iowa

"At Airport Mesa, I felt the presence of many spirits. I had a vision of my grandmother, who died many years ago. Then, at Cathedral Rock, I had a past-life vision as an [American] Indian."

S.R.
Mesa, Arizona

"While in college, I was in an automobile accident and suffered damage to my back in which several vertebrae were broken, resulting in a great many back problems and very painful arthritis. I had always accepted this as my fate, but when we were in Sedona, the thought came to me that perhaps there was a past-life connection.

"I saw myself as a handsome young man in my late teens or early twenties. I sensed I was in France, perhaps the 17th or 18th century, as transportation was by buggy. I was at a swimming place, dressed in wool knit swimming clothes that nearly covered my entire body. I was showing off to the girls, thinking I was really smart. I did a high dive off some structure and broke my back.

"The next thing I saw was myself laying in a bed in some top floor room (my bed was under the eaves). I had no visitors, and I just lay there, neither helping myself nor being useful; I willed myself to die very young.

"During the healing circle, after forgiving myself for wasting that lifetime, I sent all my concentration to my back. I have received a great relief of pain; my back is much stronger, almost to the point of being healed. Every time I feel any discomfort there, I tell myself that my back is healed, and immediately the pain becomes much less severe than it was."

H.K.
Eugene, Oregon

"I was an [American] Indian woman. I held a small child in my arms and I was worried about the men who had been gone for some time. The feeling was so feminine, it was as though I were being embraced by a huge mother presence. She was so kind and gentle and loving. I saw [a] woman with long braids, dressed in brown chamois and moccasins, smiling at me and beckoning me to follow her."

L.F.
Lake Ozark, Missouri

"I had an interesting follow-up to the past-life regression given by Don Tinling at the seminar.

"At the time of the regression, I felt I was having difficulty concentrating. Nothing was coming easily and I did not feel that I was as deeply under as everyone around me seemed to be. But I am an aspiring writer and so decided to use the time to make up a short story. I never felt, as others stated later, that it was me living an experience; I felt rather that I was viewing my character on a movie screen and that I was making it all up as I went along. (Note: It is a common reaction to feel you are making things up while in hypnosis.)

"My character was a teenager, training as a dancer in a temple. I had seen pictures of Teotihuacan and this place wasn't it, although there was a pyramid. It was near the ocean. The temple she was dancing in faced the west, and I could see the setting sun through the four columns of the entrance. There were lots of pictures on the walls.

"Her name was Almacita, and she was thrilled because of the new copper bells ornamenting her skirt. These were new to the area. She thought of Teotihuacan as being in the past, and wondered how many interesting secrets those people had known. Nobody knew secrets now and her questions about older ways were brushed aside. When Don asked what the name of the place was, 'Tellum' came to my mind.

"Later, I stopped by a Sedona bookstore. I was drawn to a book on the top shelf and needed a stool to reach it. *Mayan Ruins of Mexico in Color* was the title of the book, written by William M. Ferguson. It had a list of ruins on the cover; I'd heard of some of them, such as Palenque, Uxmal, and Chichen Itza. At the bottom of the list was one I'd never consciously heard of: Tulum. On page 195, I found a picture of a pyramid with the caption 'A Temple of the Frescoes' below it. The ocean was behind the pyramid; the temple, with four columns, was facing west. In the text, I read that copper ornaments on clothing did not come to the area until the post-classic era, around A.D. 1300; the Temple of the Frescoes, with its beautiful murals, was not built until after A.D. 1400, long after the classic period of Teotihuacan!"

N.
Post Falls, Idaho

"On Sunday morning, Shawndee and I were in bed in our room; I was relating to her my past-life regression of the night before, which I had not yet written down. We were directed to relive the happiest, proudest day of that lifetime. I was telling Shawndee that I was so proud because I had been allowed to put up my beautiful, long dark hair for my very first grown-up party. I wore a gorgeous red gown and a lovely lace mantilla in that life, and was so proud and happy.

"Suddenly, my daughter Toni, who was getting ready for the seminar, burst into the room from the dressing area waving a paper, saying, 'Read this, Mom! Just read this!'

"The written account of her past-life regression was almost word-for-word what I had just been relating to Shawndee. None of us had discussed this after the session; we had simply gone to dinner and talked of other things. It was just one of those amazing things we experienced. We don't quite understand that one, but it's still remarkable."

S.M.
Dolan Springs, Arizona

"At the Bell Rock Vortex, meditating on a past life, a vision appeared before my eyes: a brightly colored sun sign, bright yellow with spokes of gleaming white, seemed to embed itself on a rock wall. Leaning against the wall was a young . . . girl. She was in tears and very depressed. I asked in what way I could help—she seemed so alone.

"Weeping, she replied, 'I'm going to have a child, and the [father] cannot marry me. I am forced to leave my tribe and my people.'

"I asked her, 'Will you come with me and together we will raise the child?'

"As she came toward me, the vision lifted. I was then instructed to go back to Sedona where I was to purchase a certain item which I would be shown. I was to take it home to share with my daughter.

"Back in Sedona, I searched several shops and found nothing. Finally, as I entered another shop that sold mostly sand paintings, I was stumped. Sand paintings had never meant much to me, just a lot of [American] Indian symbols which I knew nothing about. I began to go through them, one at a time. Suddenly, as I stared speechlessly, one nearly stuck to my hand. It was a sun-god and feathers. In the middle of the sun was a small figure with many small, colored squares on either side of the figure. I didn't know the significance of the figures, I only knew that I had to purchase it. As I pulled out my wallet, I asked the proprietor of the store to explain its meaning to me. 'The small figure is the god of fertility,' he said, 'and the colored squares represent the rainbow of hope and happiness.' As I listened, tears filled my eyes as well as my heart, only they were tears of happiness!!

"Now I know the young [American] Indian girl is my daughter now.

I helped her through her life as [a] girl, and in this life, she has gone through the hell of cancer with me that I might live. Ten years ago, I was told I had three to nine months to live. My daughter went to a special hospital where she learned to administer certain experimental treatments which she gave me for three years. Oh, it was pure hell. She has more than repaid the love I shared with her as the [American] Indian maiden."

N.W.
Richmond, Missouri

CHAPTER 12

AUTOMATIC WRITING

As I mentioned previously, automatic writing is one of the exercises people find the most rewarding to do in the vortexes. During the Sedona Psychic Seminar, I will lead the group in an altered-state automatic writing session.

I suggest that participants contact a "wisdom entity," someone they admire who has passed over and would be capable of relating information that would assist them, either spiritually, intellectually, physically, or materially.

This involves entering a relaxed state through meditation or self-hypnosis while sitting in a comfortable position with a notepad on your lap and a pen in hand. Once relaxed, the participants open their eyes and allow their hands to write whatever comes.

Often, if nothing is immediately forthcoming, it is helpful to keep drawing circles until letters begin to appear. It is not unusual for automatic writing to be different from your own handwriting, or even for it to change from time to time, as witnessed by a participant from Fresno, California, who wished to remain anonymous: "The automatic writing brought surprises in that a new 'guide' was introduced about midway and the writing changed dramatically."

If you would like to learn more about automatic writing, we offer a 74-minute audio course, available at Hayhouse.com/downloads. Enter Product ID **6829** and Download Code **course**.

Entities contacted ranged from the "sublime to the ridiculous" as Napoleon once said. These are a few examples of automatic writings received:

"After making contact with a spirit in Boynton Canyon, I read some astrology charts with his interpretation. I placed my left hand over the chart and used my right hand for automatic writing. I would read what was being written, question where the information was in the chart, look at the chart and say to myself, 'Of course! How simple!'

"The feeling of love from this spirit was so intense that I was shaking and crying the entire time I was doing this. I received so much energy from there that I was up until 4 a.m., walking around with a flashlight at the Airport Mesa and Bell Rock Vortexes. (I slept very well and awoke completely refreshed and full of energy at 7:30.)"

Name Withheld

"For a long time, I had visualized myself as sitting on a huge reservoir of creative power, unable to tap into it because of its stone shell. During my Boynton Canyon Vortex experience, two of my guides showed up, but I resisted them because they weren't what I expected. They were a couple of jokers—slapstick jokers. I felt a slight sinking feeling of disappointment. Dignified

Masters they were not. I finally decided to acknowledge them and find out if they really were meant for me. They told me they were my guides—for a while, anyway.

"One was a man with short gray hair and a beard, rather professorial looking. When I asked his name, he answered, 'Tamur,' readily enough. But the other character, manifested as a very odd looking, slate-colored pyramid, just smiled . . . when I asked him what his name was. He and Tamur kept looking at each other, nudging each other and laughing. I couldn't believe it. Finally, he said, 'Just call me The Wedge.' 'The Wedge?' I asked, beginning to feel like a straight man. 'Yeah,' he giggled, not explaining. I was feeling somewhat bewildered by this time. I said, somewhat disappointedly, 'You're not very serious.' 'Are you?' they responded. And I had to acknowledge I had gotten what I deserved.

"They settled down somewhat, and as they both looked intently at me, Tamur asked if I really wanted 'this.' Not really knowing what 'this' was, I still felt very definitely that yes, I wanted 'this.' Whereupon The Wedge dove, headfirst, into my solar plexus. Surprised, but not alarmed, I asked Tamur, 'What's he doing? What's going on?' Tamur said, 'It's all right. He's cleansing some energies.'

"My solar plexus began to glow with an orange light—looking something like whirling molten lava edged with darker, harder crust. After a few minutes, The Wedge withdrew. I came up then, feeling peaceful and content. I believe The Wedge broke a hole in the stone shell covering my reservoir, which probably explains why I had such success in the automatic writing after that.

"Alan Vaughan advised us to contact a 'wisdom' entity, but having admired the immense talent of a man who had just passed over, I thought I would like to see what I could get from Orson Welles. I thought it might be a mistake . . . but I figured he was an individual of some higher development, so I decided to try.

"After going down very well and calling Orson, I experienced a jolt in my solar plexus and my hand proceeded to write jerkily. I have never had such a decisive physical reaction before. I was and am very pleased. This is what I/Orson wrote: 'I want to be left alone. I don't want to be bothered now. Please let me be.' I sent him white light and love and asked to please [tell me] something about how he died—I'm afraid I didn't want to let him go because I was thrilled with the contact. 'My heart failed. I have no more information.' I told him to feel free to come through me whenever he decided to manifest, and then sent him more peace and light.

"I decided to call someone I could depend on—Edgar Cayce. 'I'll help you, my dear. What would you like to know?' 'What can you tell me about myself?' I asked. 'You can begin a great work now,' he replied.

"Excited, I asked another question: 'Is there something you can tell me that will relate to all of us here?' He replied, 'Yes. I will say you have only to look to your heart's desire to find your spirit. I will come again, when you call.'

"I didn't know what else to ask, but I didn't want him to go. Edgar introduced me to an . . . entity called Ma Jong, and then departed. The . . . entity communicated, 'You will be a great inspiration to many. Do not fail them. Do what you have seen and follow your heart's desire. I will come also when asked. You are beginning.

You must clarify your thoughts and shield yourself from the confusion of life.'

"An affirmation I received was 'I am a being of light and joy. I will be a channel of blessing.' And then Ma Jong concluded, 'We are finished.'

"I'm thrilled to pieces. This is the most physical manifestation of my psychic ability I've ever had. I can look at my pages of jerky writing as proof that this is real."

C.K.
Clarkston, Michigan

"I was sharing a suite with a friend at Los Abrigados, and on Saturday, I awoke feeling very sad, that whatever had occurred during my sleep was much more pleasant than awakening at the resort. I don't know exactly how to explain it except that I wanted to go back to wherever I was. I remember only one thing, very vaguely, from that night's sleep: I remember being introduced to a guide who was going to tell me of the ways of the Hopi. I remember turning over and going back into a deep sleep.

"But that morning, at breakfast, my friend inquired as to whether I remembered anything from my dreams. I told her of my only occurrence; then she proceeded to inform me that during the night, she observed me sitting in the lotus position and chanting. (My body does not lend itself well to the lotus position.)

"Then, on Saturday afternoon, after Dick released us to visit the vortexes, my friend and I went to Airport Mesa, where I went into an altered state of consciousness and opened myself to receive automatic writing. After receiving some beautiful writing from a guide named Green Tree, I asked if he could explain what had happened the night before. The following are the words that quickly came through my hands: 'We spoke to you of our shaman ways and performed an initiation. You are one of us now and will continue to do our works as do many shamans before you. Be honest and truthful and sincere. You will spread our ways among the land.' I'll never forget the feelings I experienced in the vortex. One can see Bell Rock from Airport Mesa, and I looked over at it and kept thinking of it as 'home.'"

Name Withheld

"Most important to me is discovering my capacity for automatic writing. I successfully did this on five occasions in Sedona and have continued at home with very interesting results."

(Note: The attached message was received during the seminar exercise.)

"As part of the experiment, I specifically asked to hear from this person: 'It was preordained that I would be here to give my life to free people from bondage. In one of my previous lives, I was Moses. My purpose has always been to free people from bondage.

"'I am going to walk in very soon into a body in Africa. We have spent enough time on apartheid. It is time for freedom from all nations. There will be a change in Russia as you know it—those people are in a different kind of bondage. They will start on a path of enlightenment. It will sweep the nation, there will be nothing the government can do to stop this movement. There will also be a tremendous change throughout the world. This will be very large in the third-world nations. The United States will be turned upside down with awareness.

"'You, Janice, are to write a manual of basic information that we will send to you, for all those people who need plain, simple language to explain the concept of love and the many dimensions of what you call God. It doesn't matter what you call him. The concept is real—we are all real and all part of God and each other. The peoples of the Earth plane are finally reawakening to this remembrance. There are so many dimensions that you have forgotten but will now remember.

"'The curse on the Earth is starting to lift. The many technologies that are so great in your eyes are only a preview of the many, many things you will remember, and we will live again in Grace.'

"The many fast circles at the beginning and throughout the automatic writing is a channeling down of energy to a level which can be received by the physical body."

J.L.
Cupertino, California

"'This is for Marsha. Greetings to you, also of Lemurian stature, a wise one of old, readied once again—a kindred soul of once highest evolution. To you, Marsha, through Shirley, we tell you this! Our message to you is one of love in your recent endeavors of a very personal nature—one which Shirley is not consciously aware, but you know what is meant. You are one of the highest of the kindred and have always been so—respect yourself, your decision. You are once again on the path—your own path—do not be afraid. You have your own Masters and guides who love you and have been waiting a long time for you to open up! Be aware that we are kind, loving, and will never hurt you. Now, as to your recent and present endeavors: Do it now! You know that you are ready. All you need is confidence. Have that and you are home free! Free . . . free of thyself and into your truest nature. Remember always, you are loved by those above you and regarded in the kindest of lights. Always know this and forever seek, and you shall obtain! Farewell—we will meet you again. You belong to the Beloved. That is all!'

"I have this funny peculiarity: whenever I hear or perceive 'truth,' I either get gooseflesh, chills, and shaking, or I am moved to tears. The crying is spontaneous and can be very, very embarrassing occasionally. Anyway, Shirley got as far as 'Greetings to you, also of Lemurian stature' and I was bawling. What's really funny about this message is the 'waiting a long time for you to open up.' I grew up knowing that guides and Masters were around to help us, but I very stubbornly and vehemently stated, over and over, that I would 'do it myself,' and 'I didn't need any help.' Only recently have I yielded to the idea of consciously seeking guidance and assistance through meditations. Capricorns can be so dense sometimes, and in early life at least, seem to thrive on taking the most difficult route possible. God, am I glad I'm growing out of that phase!

"So, they really have been waiting. I have consciously and verbally pushed them away until now. Also, I have been vacillating over some decisions—three very major life changes. The message was accurate to my present needs and I did intuitively understand exactly what they were referring to as Shirley read the message. Also, Shirley got really choked up when she read the 'You are of the Beloved.' She said that when this came through her, she had the feeling of great honor, like this was a very wonderful and special distinction.

"Was the Beloved a concept of God? Love? An organization of kindred spirits? An individual? Poses some very interesting questions. Perhaps you could find out more from others. Also, was this a Lemurian term only, or is it a universally accepted word for a concept? I'd like to know.

"In the class exercises, I was able to demonstrate success in every exercise presented, which astounded me because I've never been interested in developing psychic ability. I am interested in further developing my ability to influence others to heal themselves.

"The energy of Sedona was attractive because I've recently been interested in the relationship of energy channeling in illness and chakras. I only came for that reason. All this other stuff was a complete surprise to me."

M.L.

"As I was browsing through my favorite metaphysical bookstore, about a week before the seminar, I picked up a certain book, flipped through the pages, and put it down again, continuing to browse. For some reason, I came back again to that book and realized that I wanted it even though it was not the type of book I would ordinarily buy. I never had an inclination to read the book, but seemed to intuitively understand what was in it. I always kept the book on a night stand in the bedroom where I do my trance work. What was even more unusual was that I packed that book to take to Sedona—2,600 miles way!

"I had just spent several years dealing with a medical condition that defied diagnosis. It was an exasperating experience, cost a hundred thousand dollars, and led me to the notion of writing a book to be used in medical schools concerning the improvement of doctor/patient communications.

"I had never participated in automatic writing prior to this time; however, I kept an open mind. As we were guided into trance, I chose the wise character of Albert Schweitzer, even though I did not know much about Dr. Schweitzer except that he was well-known for his medical work in Africa. I came to understand much more about this man.

"Dr. Schweitzer: 'Be sure to tell them to remember the patient is of most importance, to set aside personal feelings and concentrate their energies on that person. This method will bring much success and happiness to any doctor in the medical field.' I asked, 'Will you help me?' Dr. Schweitzer: 'Yes, I will be there to help you, just call on me.'

"Me: 'Is there any special preparation?' Dr. Schweitzer: 'No, just speak from your experience and from the heart.' Me: 'Will the book reach the right people?' Dr. Schweitzer: 'Yes, we on the other side will see that it does.' Me: 'May I begin soon?' Dr. Schweitzer: 'Yes, just as soon as you feel you are ready for the experience.' Me: 'Is there one quality that every doctor can use to treat every patient?' Dr. Schweitzer: 'Yes—love. It is so simple but the hardest of chores for most men. Let your book center around this theme.' Me: 'Thank you, Albert.' Dr. Schweitzer: 'Best wishes to you. Tell Norman I'm OK.'

"As the conversation finished, it was as though Dr. Schweitzer and I became one spirit, blending with the universal energy. At that instant, an avalanche of knowledge was available to me. The seven-year medical situation was of a karmic nature with its purpose to bring me to where I am now: studying metaphysics, writing of the experience to lend a helping hand to advance those in the medical profession, and realizing my own unlimited capabilities.

"As trite as it may sound, I am not the same person who went to Sedona; I am on a new journey."

S.A.M.
Granby, Connecticut

CHAPTER 13

OTHER PSYCHIC IMPRESSIONS

In addition to the different types of energy manifestations we have already recounted, many seminar participants wrote of various other impressions and occurrences that happened while they were in Sedona and the energy vortexes. These are a sampling.

"I came here to make contact with my ex-husband, who died two years ago. He was my soulmate. This was accomplished in Boynton Canyon with tears, anguish, [and] then happiness for both of us, and release and understanding."

Name Withheld

"On the way into Boynton Canyon, I received a thought: *Take some rocks.* 'Which ones?' I asked. The thought said, *You'll know when you see them.* I walked for a while and then came upon four small rocks lined up side by side. I saw no other rocks lined up like that. When I picked them up, I knew that three of my friends could not get to the canyon; these rocks were for them.

"Later that afternoon, I met my friends and told them, before they could say anything, that I knew they couldn't make it to Boynton Canyon, and the spirits had told me to take some rocks for them. They were surprised and overwhelmed with joy when I gave them the rocks."

J.C.H.
Lynn, Massachusetts

"I began to meditate in a yoga position, facing out over the valley. I saw a young [American] Indian [man] seated opposite me, smiling and friendly. I felt very powerful. He welcomed me, and we sat observing each other in a friendly communion of spirits; it was like filling my soul with peaceful energy and love. I began to feel very loved and loving.

"When it was time to leave, I felt charged with energy and peace. The psychic processes we did that day were very successful for me; I had not done anything like that before."

C.T.
San Diego, California

"Sedona is the place where I was able, on one special day, to find peace and tranquility to help guide my life.

"On the second day of Chanukah, my grandmother had given me a pyramid-shaped crystal to wear on my necklace. She went on to explain that when I went to Arizona with my parents that winter, I should carry the crystal to help concentrate the energies in the vortexes of Sedona, but at that time I could not appreciate the crystal's intrinsic value.

"Although spending a day at Sedona did not appeal to me, I felt compelled to honor my grandmother's request to experience it with an open mind. The first several stops were as I had expected—boring. Then we arrived at the vortex area. For some reason, I felt an urge to leave the others and go to the rushing stream I could hear not far away. As I approached the stream, the sun warmed my wind-blown face and enticed me to sit by the shore. When I sat on a welcoming boulder, I remembered to take off the crystal my grandmother had given me. Placing the crystal on my third eye (middle forehead), I began to meditate. I had seen a film on Sedona the day prior to our arrival, which described effective methods of relaxation.

"I sat by the shore for over an hour; the time passed quickly. As I meditated, I felt a sense of oneness with everything around me. It was as though I could communicate with nature and even God. I could not help but smile as I sat there; suddenly, I realized how it felt to transcend the normal plane of existence. The seemingly eccentric works of Ralph Waldo Emerson and Henry David Thoreau now made sense. I was able to share with them this divine perception of spirituality. As I left my meditation, I promised to always remember the feeling of tranquility and to return to it if I felt anger or tension in my life.

"When I returned to the shore, I realized the crystal had stayed on my forehead without assistance, defying gravity's pull. I removed the crystal and felt how warm it had become. My grandmother was right; with both the natural properties of the crystal formation and the mystical form of the pyramid, I was able to concentrate the proven energies of the vortex. I then walked back to rejoin my parents for the continuation of the tour. I was exhausted when we returned to the jeep. It was, however, a peaceful exhaustion which caused me to smile all through the remainder of our journey.

"I will never forget that day at Sedona; it has given me insight to peaceful existence in this sometimes crazy world."

S.M.
St. Petersburg, Florida

"At Bell Rock, I climbed to a plateau where I sat in meditation. Leaning against the rock, I began to feel intense heat moving through my body. I felt several electric shocks go through my body.

"Then I saw inside the rock a platform with several colored lights around it. There was a large crystal at the base of the platform and, as the heat grew stronger, the crystal broke into several small fragments, dissipated, and turned into rays of color. The waves of color then began to move toward the center of the platform and merged with the large crystal at its base. When this process was complete, I felt a tremendous sense of peace and well-being, my hearing became more acute and my perception more vivid."

S.V.
Douglas, Alaska

"I started getting pictures of the old civilization; then an inner voice said that this was not my purpose to see. My purpose was to restore my spirit and become one with the land and I would be renewed in energy and life. I felt the vibrations of the ground and the most wonderful sense of peace. I left the vortex feeling touched and changed."

J.L.L.

"I was able to reopen my automatic writing abilities in a much clearer manner. I received immediate answers to my questions; it was like a loving reunion surrounded by all my guides. I also had the experience of seeing a beautiful, fantastic aura of one of the people accompanying me."

S.L.

"I felt drawn only to the Courthouse Rock Vortex. Of my first visit, I only remember coming out of trance with my face and neck wet . . . apparently, I'd had quite a good cry though I didn't remember it.

"On the second visit, I received the following affirmation: 'Joy is the essence of my being, illuminating all I see. I am open to all healing powers, inner visions, and perfect sight. I am complete, perfect, and whole. I am indeed one with all.'"

J.B.

"Forming an arc between ourselves and another in the group that we wanted to meet, I visualized a light connecting myself and someone whom I had wanted to meet but not been able to meet all weekend. He immediately came from across the room to be my partner for the next exercise. I wonder—maybe I should write a book on 'how to meet men'!?!"

M.P.
Virginia Beach, Virginia

RELATIONSHIPS

Sharon Boyd decided to see what effect Sedona had on relationships and reported her findings in an article titled "Sedona: The Path of the Heart," which ran in Issue 45 of my magazine, *Master of Life*:

> To experience love for another person and to feel loved is possibly the most intense human desire. Through the ages, human thought has concentrated upon the issue of love and relationships.
>
> Though there are many kinds of love—the tender love of a mother for her child, the devoted love of home and family, the staunch love of country, the sincere love of ideals and philosophy—it is the passionate love experienced by two souls drawn to each other that stirs the imagination and ignites the most intense interest. Great feats have been accomplished in the name of love as well as dark deeds of passion. Much has been written about love—what love is, how to look for love, how to recognize love when you find it, how to nurture the love you have, and how to release with love when necessary.

Because love—being loving, expressing love, and experiencing love or the lack of love—is the universal condition, it is present wherever people are. This is just as true in Sedona as anywhere else. However, because of its energy vortexes, Sedona magnifies the experience of love. What many people who have visited Sedona in their quest for psychic development and fulfillment have experienced regarding their love relationships is related in the following stories.

"My interest in psychic phenomena started with a very powerful and frightening psychic experience. A woman for whom I had developed very strong emotional ties ended a . . . relationship with me and, shortly thereafter, began a relationship with a long-time friend of mine. [They] made great efforts to keep their relationship a secret from me [to spare] my feelings. While I had no tangible . . . evidence that they were involved with each other, an intuitive sense told me with remarkably strong clarity that they were.

"A sequence of events [led] me to explore deeper into psychic and spiritual realms. Among these events was my learning of Sedona. I first heard of the place from a college friend. . . . From the very first time [they] described Sedona, I sensed that I was meant to go there.

"As far as my dealing with the love triangle relationship, I took steps and made progress, but was unable to reach my ultimate goal for many months. Even before I reached Sedona, I knew that the place to go to carry out this resolution to completion was the Bell Rock Vortex. . . . Shortly after my arrival in town, I climbed a little more than three-quarters of the way up Bell Rock and wrote a letter [that] contained statements concerning my own painful feelings and what I perceived to be insensitivity on their part in the way they handled the situation. . . . Upon completing the letter, I wrote and recited a prayer on their behalf.

"I followed my experience at Bell Rock with a visit to Airport Mesa. I hiked around to the east side of the lower hill, where the lights of West Sedona were blocked and the view of the starlit, moonless sky was spectacular. I tapped the positive masculine energy of the vortex and drew it into my body and soul, concentrating on enhancing my own positive masculine qualities and strengthening my desirability and attractiveness. . . .

While this may sound like an exploitative and superficial desire, my true purpose during this meditation was to strengthen and support myself in my search for a close, loving, caring, and meaningful relationship with a woman who [would be] genuinely compatible with me. . . . The word combination I used during the meditation session, "warmth, comfort, security, fulfillment," certainly reflects a desire for that kind of intimate love, not simply a shallow fantasy. . . .

"While silently chanting that word combination, I lay stretched out on a flat rock surface high above the mesa. I drew the energy from below me up through my feet, and the energy from the hill above and behind me through the top of my head. [After] I did this for about 15 minutes . . . I found myself reveling joyously in my masculinity. . . .

"The next day, I went to Boynton Canyon to meditate. During this meditation, I heard a medley of voices talking. The wind suddenly started to blow down from the east wall of the canyon behind me, growing steadily from a whistle to a howl to a frightful roar. The voices said, 'Feel the power, energy, and life force of the wind. From now on, every time you feel the wind, you will sense the spiritual force of it. You will be conscious of the force entering into you as the wind blows over you. You are not going back where you came from. You will never go back there again. The physical place will be the same—you will not. Everyone around you will perceive the change. You will grow to incredible lengths, heights, and strengths you cannot believe of yourself now.'

"At this point, light rain began to fall. 'Drink in the rain, the power and glory of it contained in every drop. Expose yourself fully to the rain and the wind, let them sweep over you and cover you completely, feel their energy and radiance fill you up. Just as with the wind, every time you feel the rain, you will feel the power, energy, and life force in every drop; you will be conscious of it entering and filling you, making you brighter and stronger. Feel the radiance enter you now.'

"I was keenly conscious of the power in the wind and rain filling me up and enveloping me, covering me, and building higher and higher. I felt it flowing out into the canyon, filling up the basin below, and rising up against the canyon walls.

"I knew that, from then on, I would always sense the energy and power in the rain and wind, as well as in the sunlight, snow, fog, and all other kinds of climatic conditions. I would sense it in the sound of birds singing and insects buzzing, the fragrance of flowers and trees and in all the infinite bounty of nature. I would always be aware of all these things instilling strength and light in me, and my mind raced with ecstasy at this prospect.

"I said a profound prayer of thanks to God and the spirit forces for all my experiences at the Sedona vortexes. On my way back, the sun emerged, and a comforting, cooling wind blew off and on. I could feel in both of them what I was told I would be able to, and have felt it ever since."

D.S.
Brooklyn, New York

"Upon meditating, I asked for specific information about a lifetime shared with a friend of mine whom I'll call Jim. I regressed to an [American] Indian incarnation and received some information, but it was sketchy. One of my guides came through during automatic writing, and I received some information that would be important for Jim to know. I have an existing, well-established means of communicating with this guide that works well for us. I realized it wasn't necessary to try to squeeze our communications into the format of automatic writing, so I set my pen and paper down, and reverted to the old way of just 'knowing.'

"I now understand that this friend and I have shared many lifetimes, always acting as a catalyst for the other's spiritual growth. We weave in and out of each other's lives, always causing the other to stretch spiritually. We plant seeds for the other's growth, and in doing that, we grow ourselves. The times when we've both been on the same spiritual level or realm have been very joyful but short-lived because we're always tossing a spiritual baton for the other to catch.

"My guide instructed me in some simple rituals to cleanse and recharge a small token my friend gave me. It will be sent back to him, and the baton is tossed again."

L.A.
Phoenix, Arizona

"My experience in Sedona was very emotional and intense. As you stated during the seminar, relationships could become richer or break apart because of the energy around Sedona. I can testify to the truth in your statement.

"My fiancé and I found ourselves dealing with some issues that could affect the continuation of our relationship. This occurred on Friday afternoon. By noon on Saturday, we had resolved these issues and we became closer than ever before. I personally experienced a catharsis, releasing emotions that were concealed for a long time. The subsequent meditations helped me realize the truth about an aspect of my personality that I did not even recognize. There were moments when I said to myself, 'I do not even know who I am anymore!' But by Sunday afternoon, I was beginning to recognize myself again.

"I also felt very intense sexual desires during my stay in Sedona. During lovemaking, I felt a higher level of energy and experienced orgasms beyond description. There is a very definite connection between sexuality and the energy emitting from the area around Sedona."

D.P.
Aurora, Colorado

"My boyfriend and I were fighting almost the entire time we were in Sedona. At two o'clock Saturday morning, I woke him and made him go to the Boynton Canyon Vortex in the rain. We had a very powerful emotional experience where we could both see the other's point of view and also the outcome of our future together. It was a most healing time for our two hearts. I felt very blessed."

C.S.
Winnemucca, Nevada

"My girlfriend and I visited Boynton Canyon. We decided to meditate separately for a while, [and] then to join hands and meditate together.

"Since our relationship was in its early stages, we decided to meditate on this question together: 'What do we need to know about each other?'

"During this meditation, I 'saw,' on the inside of my eyelids, each quality of my girlfriend as if it were carved in huge letters on the stone wall of the canyon. My guides explained each quality to me if any needed explanation.

Then they told me many more things about her and our relationship, which she later confirmed over dinner. She also received many things about me during meditation that she had not known before. They were all true."

L.C.
Phoenix, Arizona

"While in the Boynton Canyon Vortex with an old friend, my husband, and a new friend from Sedona, we walked through a dried riverbed over large slabs of sandstone. My companions were properly outfitted for a stroll through the canyon, I was not—the shoes I was wearing were not the most appropriate for hiking. Although I did not complain and was able to keep up with the others, I was not feeling too happy.

"As I struggled to keep up, I noticed that I was picking up negative feelings . . . feelings of intense hatred emanated from my old friend. I tried to ignore the feelings, but the more I ignored them, the more intense they became.

"Suddenly, my friend came running up the path. Pushing aside a thorny branch, she let it snap back at me without warning, scratching my hand. As I nursed my bleeding hand, I growled, 'Thanks a lot.' Childlike, she ran off, whining, 'I didn't do it on purpose.'

"I began to see how childish she was, something I had never consciously realized before in all the years I had known her. I slowly became aware that I was attracted to her because of those childlike ways, and that I acted like a mother to her. And I knew this could not go on.

"I also began to pick up feelings that she was attracted to my husband, noticing at a deep level that she was becoming a seductress and my husband was also attracted to her. There was no hiding anyone's feelings—they were right there, out in the open. I realized how out of control I was, how I've struggled to control people and situations.

"Although the experience in the Boynton Canyon Vortex wasn't what I would call a pleasant experience, it was a cleansing experience, which was a new beginning for me in learning more about the patterns I've been holding in my subconscious for lifetimes. It was also the beginning of my clearing the air with my friend so our relationship could take a healthier turn.

"The next time I go to Sedona, I will go by myself. I want to experience the stillness and energy without having to go through any more traumatic experiences or having to handle someone else's strong emotions.

"I felt like the whole Sedona area was a vortex, that the air was caressing, healing. All in all, I had a wonderful week in Sedona. It has changed my whole life; I no longer want to be in control of my relationships, and I am starting to really listen to my feelings and express them."

A.R.
Mountain Lakes, New Jersey

As evidenced in the stories above, Sedona can have a powerful impact on the soul's expression and experience of love. Of the three aspects of love—spiritual, sexual, and emotional—the spiritual element is probably the element most magnified by the power of the Sedona vortexes. Good relationships can be enhanced and experienced with a joyousness sometimes missing in daily life; changes necessary to improve relationships can be seen more clearly; relationships that have evolved in different directions can be released more easily.

The more letters and stories we read from those who have visited the power vortexes, the more amazed we become at the integrative qualities the vortexes display— developing psychic abilities, encouraging the body's own healing processes, soothing wounded spirits, and stimulating loving feelings.

And so the visions, the past-life memories, the meditative insights, the healings, and the energy continue. We could probably provide an endless supply of reports of vortex experiences, but that's not the idea. The idea is to make people aware that these things do exist and we can experience them for ourselves.

Your own experiences in the Sedona energy vortexes would surpass any that you've read here because that experience would be unique; it would have meaning for you alone. When we seek to develop our psychic talents, what we are doing is seeking to improve ourselves, our relationships, and the quality of our lives in all aspects.

Hopefully, if you haven't already, you will get a chance to visit Sedona and experience the magnificent energy for yourself. But, if not, realize that all the experiments and experiences you've read about here can also be manifested in your own home. A trip to Sedona isn't necessary to try automatic writing, past-life regressions, hypnosis programming, or meditation. Don't use the lack of vortex energy as an excuse not to develop your own psychic abilities.

CHAPTER 14

WHAT HAPPENS AT A PSYCHIC SEMINAR?

As a little background, you might want to know what happens at a Sedona Psychic Seminar—individuals' reactions to it and how it seems to act as a catalyst for the myriad experiences reported in this book.

The seminar is structured for personal psychic experiences and development in such areas as telepathy, trance channeling, clairvoyance, psychometry, automatic writing, remote viewing, and psychokinesis. It also includes past-life regressions and much more. Well-known psychics and metaphysical practitioners usually co-train the seminars with me.

Since the Sedona area, particularly around the vortexes, expands energy, including psychic energy, participants who have never experienced psychic input or ability have been absolutely amazed at what they could do psychically after the proper instructions and preparation. Once you have learned to test the vortex energy, then activate and expand it, the psychic potentials of your vortex experiences are greatly enhanced.

In our very first Sedona Psychic Seminar in May of 1984, 96 percent of the participants reported successful results in the psychic experimental sessions and in the energy vortex areas. After several Sedona Psychic Seminars with similar successes, I became convinced that we could take the actual training sessions a giant step further.

At the next Sedona Psychic Seminar, with the energy of the area intensifying the participants' latent abilities, we conducted new and highly successful telepathy and clairvoyant experiments. As the seminar progressed, participants were assigned to do psychic readings on each other. The success rate was phenomenal, especially for the individuals conducting the readings who didn't realize the depths of their own psychic abilities.

Of the 253 people who attended, only 21 were professionally involved in some form of metaphysical practice. According to our research, 80 percent rated themselves as having no psychic ability, "but I want to develop it" or "a little psychic ability." Almost every state in the country was represented, plus two foreign countries. The average participant had two or three years of college and many had professional degrees. At the end of the seminar, we passed out follow-up sheets. One of the things asked on the follow-up was, "Please relate your most interesting vortex experience."

The following responses are typical of the comments I received.

"Since I wasn't sure what to expect and was very skeptical, I tried to focus on keeping an open mind. I was surprised at the success I had in most of the exercises and how well a person 'hit me on the head' with the 'fairy tale' exercise. I got in touch with a lot of issues inside me—whether it came from guides, a higher power, or whomever."

Name Withheld
Houston, Texas

"Thank you for validating my right to be psychic! I picked up the three symbols you sent to the group with an ease that excited me. I also picked up the picture of a black and white dog during the transmission and wonder at this still."

Name Withheld
Burbank, California

"This is my second Sedona Psychic Seminar; it's habit-forming. Because the environment and personalities are very comfortable, I was able to open up—my awareness has become so much keener. The psychometry exercise and reading each other were very successful for me. It is finally getting to the point where psychic ability feels 'natural,' somewhat like moving from kindergarten to grammar school, with a long way to go, but progress is quite evident!"

S.T.
Lawndale, California

"During the psychometry experiments, I was astounded when I gave my impressions to our little group. I really didn't know whose question was on the folded paper I held. I know I do automatic writing easily, but I didn't have much confidence with being able to give an accurate mini-reading on such short notice. However, when I finished, the girl on my right burst out that I had exactly expressed her innermost thoughts and desires, [and] described her completely. She was amazed because she'd never had the nerve to admit these ambitions to anyone. I'd just gone with what came to me."

S.M.
Dolan Springs, Arizona

"I suppose I was a bit skeptical at first and thought that I was making everything up. During the automatic writing session, the gentleman that I 'read for' told me that chances were one in a million that I could have zeroed in like I did. I have more confidence in my abilities now and will follow my intuition more often. Truly an incredible experience."

M.P.
Virginia Beach, Virginia

"The seminar was not only informative but showed me that psychic abilities are our right. I'd believed others had this talent but not me. The seminar showed me it is not only possible, but you really have to work hard *not* to use it."

R.L.J.
Dallas, Texas

The usual flow of the seminar goes something like this: The participants are conditioned through altered-state and other sessions to perceive psychically, and then are taught techniques to use in the seminar room and the vortexes. After a "vortex orientation" on Saturday in which I explain how to use the vortex energy and discuss the dangers involved, the participants are free to explore the four vortexes on their own. In the evenings, we often do past-life group regressions or use other altered-state techniques to explore and discuss the day's vortex experiences.

On Sunday, when psychic abilities are peaking, we conduct tests to allow participants to judge their own psychic accuracy. Most are amazed that they can do valid "readings" on strangers and receive information through automatic writing. Sunday afternoon covers psychometry and healing, often with incredible results. The Healing Circle Meditation closes the seminar.

Participants frequently stay over for a few days after the seminar to continue their vortex experiences with heightened psychic abilities.

To give you a more intimate view: Shortly after the first Sedona Psychic Seminar, Sharon Boyd compiled information from participants for a report in Issue 21 of *Self-Help Update* (Note: *Self-Help Update* was the previous title of my magazine, *Master of Life/WINNERS*) titled "The Voices of the Vortex." In it, she detailed events ranging from the participants' psychic experiences to encounters with a rattlesnake.

> One of the most exciting seminars we've done recently was the Psychic Seminar in Sedona this past spring. Dick Sutphen, assisted by Alan Vaughan, guided over 100 participants during the fun-filled three-day seminar, exploring psychic potentials through a variety of awareness-expanding sessions, group exercises, experiments, and hypnosis.
>
> Sedona is a small town located approximately 100 miles from Phoenix. In the area is one of the legendary "power spots," or energy vortexes, mentioned in many different legends and tales from varying [sic] cultural backgrounds. There are said to be four of these energy power spots in the world;

psychic and metaphysical impressions and experiences can be enhanced through contact with these psychometric areas.

One of the legends about the Sedona power spot is that it is the site of an ancient Lemurian city. During an outing to the vortex site, the group was asked to be especially sensitive to the vibrations and see if their impressions concurred with the legend.

Dick gave them specific instructions as well as a gentle posthypnotic suggestion that any disturbance or background noise would only serve to deepen and enhance their altered state rather than distracting them. They were told to allow their minds to be open and receptive to the images, neither blocking them nor straining for them, but to just let the impressions flow and trust what they received.

The energy at the vortex was terrific; one woman confessed, several days after the seminar, that she was so charged up that everyone she touched was "shocked" and her electrostatic air cleaner would pop like crazy whenever she was around it.

All were excited by the adventure; several people agreed to let us print their experiences in the magazine so our readers could share in the fantastic energy, too. Not everyone wrote their experiences and impressions down for us—some felt they needed time to sort out their impressions, others weren't sure they had received anything, but those who did share with us had some experiences that were incredible.

A lot of [American] Indians came through in the communications with the vortexes; they indicated that the area was a very powerful energy area, revered and guarded by [them]. There was also confirmation that a Lemurian city had once stood upon the spot.

R.C., from Escondido, California, had an interesting confirmation of the city; he meditated for contact with a leader of the time of Lemuria, and shared these impressions with us: "I was a spirit leader in the time of Lemuria. Many people question if it existed at all. I tell you, it is an absolute fact!

"Many thousands of years ago, on this location, was the temple of the highest order of the Lemurian priesthood. For centuries after the demise of Lemuria, it was recognized as the source of the earth's power in this part of the world; each succeeding civilization has been led to recognize this fact.

"The [American] Indians kept the area as sacred ground; only medicine men ever ventured near. Its significance has been known in recent years only by a few people, but the area is now coming into major importance once again.

"Lemuria was a lush and verdant country of tropical climate—fruit and all manner of vegetation grew in abundance and the people had the opportunity to become very spiritually advanced. This they chose to ignore; even so, their general advancement was far superior to that of most people today.

"They became embroiled in competition with the Atlanteans, as your present knowledge indicates. The quest was acquisition of land—a dream not yet purged from the minds of men even in your generation.

"They were extremely advanced in many ways—the printed word, medicine, and what you call psychic knowledge (teleportation, telepathy, and precognition as well as healing), were ordinary occurrences in all households. Unfortunately, some abused these powers even as Russia is attempting to do today."

At this point, R.V.'s reverie was interrupted by the spectacle of a tow truck preparing to haul everyone's cars away. A cry went up from the crowd, and people began to run toward their cars. This was a disturbance that would definitely alter their state!

A.V. said that he was in communication with a long-time guide when [he] told him, "go take care of it." Alan opened his eyes and saw a yellow Camaro being hoisted up in the air. As he started toward the tow truck, he heard his guide whisper once more, and the tow truck immediately let the car down.

During the seminar, A.V. also channeled an entity he had never actually contacted before but who had been described to him by three mediums 16 years before! "Li Sung" made his appearance suddenly in response to a couple whom [he] had just met. "Li Sung" gave much past-life information concerning the couple and [him], as well as giving other attendees valuable and interesting information about their past lives.

At one point, the flow of impressions and surging energy were so powerful and strong at the vortex that one woman burst spontaneously into song, channeling powerful inspiration from the ancient Lemurian vibrations.

R.B., standing nearby, was so moved by the song that she asked why she was unable to unblock her throat so that she, too, could sing.

"I was in a self-induced hypnotic trance at the time," R.B. said. "I started going back through my life, remembering incidents about singing. All the incidents that came up were concerned with my inability to sing.

"Finally, I saw a picture of myself as a little girl of eight or nine, singing in a church choir. It was a fundamentalist Baptist church. The preacher's sermon was about how God punished sinners and which sins got the worst punishment. He finished by saying, 'Let us all sing a hymn to the greater glory of God.' At that point, the little girl who I was at the time said, 'I won't sing to a God who does that to people,' and I closed down and quit singing.

"I could physically feel my throat relax as I understood what had happened. When I opened my mouth to sing, I could feel how free my muscles had become. It was a wonderful experience of freedom for me." And R.B. joined her voice to that of the woman, singing in beautiful harmony and wordless joy.

R.F. received information during automatic writing concerning the ancient city and the song: "This area is holy and spiritual. There is an ancient city here. For your purpose, call it Lemuria. You are all citizens of Lemuria and have agreed to meet here regularly to maintain and increase the spirit of this place. Come back here if ever you doubt your strength. You were wise to come here to gain insight into your abilities. This is your ancient home and it is still here. The song you heard today was actually being sung in a temple in Lemuria; we wanted to share it with you in appreciation of your renewing the energy. The energy exchange is a two-way process—you give as you receive and we need your energy to continue. Believe in your power and it increases.

"Though hard for you to understand and believe, Lemuria is now, and you are a part of both. Your collective mission is to share the love and wisdom so that it spreads. As it spreads, our power and abilities shall increase.

"Trust in yourselves and what you are doing. It is right and appropriate that you are all here at this time. We needed your energy and you have done well . . . we are back on track."

R.P., a calm, quiet man, related that he has always had a persistent, recurring fear of having people become dependent upon him. While raising his children, that fear became a constant source of conflict with his wife. He wanted the children to be able to fend for themselves as early as possible and his wife, rather naturally, thought that it was not right. Her mothering instinct was offended by this "necessity" her husband deemed so important for the children to learn.

This fear even carried over to his business life; he had always tried to avoid the spotlight, preferring instead to work behind the scenes. Many people, aware of his talents, had tried to coax him into exercising his leadership abilities but in vain. R.P. said, "I know I can do this, but so far I'm not able to do this."

In the meditation regression that Sunday, R.P. asked for the cause of his obsession. "I went back to a past life in Kauai, Hawaii, in the middle 1700s," [he] related. "I was a Kahuna, or priest, who had many people who were dependent on me for consultation and spiritual leadership.

"As my reputation grew, I became more arrogant and self-centered. Eventually, I lost contact with my God-self and began to feel invincible and omnipotent. I had become drunken with my power.

"When my advice was sought regarding an upcoming battle with King Kamehameha [Note: Kamehameha was king from 1810–1819], I believed my power would overcome the enemy. I advised against extensive preparations, believing, in my arrogance, that it really was unnecessary. I had been listened to for so many years that I began to listen to myself.

"In the battle, the entire village was slaughtered; I fled into the mountains, where I died a lonely death."

Realizing the cause of his fear will allow [him] to begin to apply his energies in ways that can be even more productive than before. "This has made me very much aware of the fine line between the use and abuse of power," R.P. said after the seminar.

Not all of the inspiration dealt with the Lemurian city or answers to personal queries; one of the impressions received by A.M. was a beautiful message from an [American] Indian guide: "The winds and the fire and sacred waters and Old Mother Earth have and know the power of the universe, and as unending as the wheel, play and replay the message over and over again as the sons of sons before me have and as I have and as my sons of sons shall do— gathering at a power spot and recognizing the power of the universe, bending as the young saplings do when wearing the wind, we will learn by the experience. But the giant oak that has been around a long time will stand staunch against the wind; it will break many times without learning the lesson. To live in harmony with the world, you must learn to bend with your surroundings and love and respect all things as yourself; if you cannot, then the wheel will rotate—another time, another plane—and you will be required to learn the lessons again as it has been and how it shall be."

And so the long weekend flashed by; the eagerly awaited three days of psychic exploration seemed, when over, to have been all too brief.

One group, reluctant to end the experience, went back to the vortex site; they believed there was more they needed to discover. At the site, they began searching, moving rocks and pushing aside boulders. One particular area seemed to broadcast intense feelings to them; they were determined to push a large boulder aside, hoping to find a cave, perhaps, of the ancient ones.

Struggling and straining, they managed to move the huge rock.

"S-s-s-s-s." With a flick of its tail, a small rattle-snake slithered out of the opening the boulder had concealed and glared at the humans, as if in warning. A long moment passed—then the snake turned and vanished into the sands.

An omen, perhaps? Maybe the snake was a guardian, then again, maybe not. A message L.S. received indicates there is yet much to be discovered in the vortex area: "Wisdom from all ages, past and future, can be found here; remove blocks and anyone can find. Wisdom is available; this place is but one nugget in a whole strand of stones. It is man's choice to pick one place to let down barriers and give reverence and find solace. Magic is in the mind of the maker—when one has made magic one place, it is easier for others to follow."

And so ended an exciting weekend filled with adventure making and following magic.

About six months later, Sharon Boyd did a follow-up report on the long-term effects of the vortex energy on the participants of [this] psychic seminar, with some interesting findings. In "The Vortex Revisited," Sharon explored the results of experiments with rocks taken from the vortexes and how the seminar affected people's lives:

What are the long-term effects of exposure to the psychometric influences of a large energy vortex? Does this energy impress itself upon the surrounding rocks, plants, water . . . and can these effects be transferred to people?

We had already related the immediate results, incidents, and impressions of the vortex experience, and thought it would be interesting to see what the effects of the seminar were months later.

We devised and sent out a questionnaire to those who [had] attended. The results were both impressive and exciting, underscoring confidence in the knowledge that we are all psychic. The Sedona Psychic Seminar stimulated new directions in transformation growth, resulting in intensified awareness for all who [had] attended. Reported increases in abilities already possessed as well as new abilities obtained through the exercises taught at the seminar included easier dream recall, greater healing ability, telepathy, precognition, automatic writing, and channeling.

Approximately 83 percent of the respondents indicated that they already possessed some degree of psychic ability or had psychic experiences prior to the seminar; almost 100 percent reported a greatly intensified awareness of abilities that in several cases, they had not realized they possessed prior to attending.

Not surprisingly, the best results were obtained by those who regularly practiced the techniques they learned—ideally on a daily basis, though weekly practice yielded good results. Psychic abilities appear to be stimulated by regular usage, proving that, like many other learned abilities, practice makes—if not perfect—at least improved.

In about a quarter of the cases, new contacts were established at the vortex site and were frequently continued after the seminar. M.L.P., channeling Edgar Cayce through automatic writing, received this message concerning Dick Sutphen: "He is a warrior who is learning, but he is a good man. He has opened doors for many that no one else could. He has done much good."

One of the most intriguing aspects of the seminar lay in the effect of material from the vortex on people and surroundings. The majority of the attendees removed nothing from the site, but many of those who did reported some amazing results. (Note: We are not encouraging wholesale destruction of the vortex site by irresponsible souvenir seekers, but we feel that a small stone, pebble, leaf, or twig cannot affect the vast energy of the vortex if permission is first obtained from the vortex spirits.)

M.F. told us, "I took two rocks from the spot where I felt the greatest energy. I keep the rocks in my kitchen; whenever I feel depression or stress, I hold one in each hand above my head in a 'star' position. Now, this sounds stupid, but when I do this, all the bad feelings are gone—period—just gone in a flash!"

No, this does not sound stupid. T.C. Lethbridge has written much about stone imprinting—the impression of energy upon rock—that have carried their psychometric charges throughout millennia. These effects are greatly magnified in areas around ley lines and energy vortexes, such as the one at Sedona, and have been written about by John Michell in *The View Over Atlantis* and *The New View Over Atlantis*, and J. Havelock Fidler in *Ley Lines*.

N.H. related the details of an interesting experiment she conducted: "I broke a couple of rocks up and put them around my plants. They doubled in growth in two weeks. I put some of the rocks around plants that were nearly dead; they're healthy and huge now. I found keeping the rocks in the sun keeps them active."

She also performed tests using the rocks with friends: one who suffered from severely debilitating migraines, the other from insomnia following painful back surgery. N.H. reported that her friend's migraines vanished within minutes after holding the rocks. A piece of rock under the pillow of the insomnia sufferer alleviated her sleeplessness and encouraged the back to heal in half the normal time following surgery.

Further testing revealed that vortex water—obtained by a process similar to that used to produce flower essences and gem elixirs—produced the same beneficial results as the actual vortex material itself. This indicates that the energy absorbed by an object in the vortex can be transferred to another medium easily, rather like charging a battery. N.H. is eagerly planning further testing of vortex materials' effects upon vegetable growth.

These effects are not limited to plant growth and pain alleviation: P.B. and B.B. report a phenomenal increase in "good luck" affecting all aspects of their lives. "We took two small stones," they told us. "Our good luck, improved marriage, dramatically improved business, and income make us wonder if there is a relationship. Who knows? But we sure wouldn't give up those two stones! During the past six months, our income has nearly doubled—in surprising, unpredictable ways."

Of course, these results are not due exclusively to the effects of the Sedona stones; much of their "good luck" should be attributed to the increased awareness the seminar generated.

In J.H.'s opinion, the most valuable result of the seminar was "the great sense of peace and oneness which the group generated. I think that together we magnified the potential of the vortex." Another woman stated, "I realized I could do a lot more psychically than I thought I could, and I had been doing so long before the seminar."

A.T.'s comment synthesized the general attitude toward the psychic seminar: "I understand and have complete faith in everyone's ability to use their psychic abilities. It is not merely a gift bestowed on a few. I accept and expect my life to flow psychically. When I ask the universe for something, I get it. The seminar has made me very clear about what I want and ask for. I feel a real unity with the universe now, a feeling I did not have before. I feel very comfortable with the concept of death, or passing over to the spirit planes . . . my life runs more smoothly and clearly. In general, I have a much deeper understanding of the nature of reality."

L.H. commented, "At the time, I didn't think I got much from it, but now I am becoming more self-assured. It's hard to explain . . . my power of positive thinking is much stronger, beginning to come to me more and more."

M.F. enthused, "No experience could top the seminar! That was minute-by-minute amazement—hours crammed with one incredible happening after another. Upon returning home, I was eager to try out my new abilities on everyone." More seriously, she added, "That is, until I took a friend's hand to 'read' for her. I saw and felt only a terrible sadness that was hard to relate. Frankly, it scared me. I learned in that flash what a responsibility psychic ability is."

Indeed it is . . . but used in a mature way by self-aware individuals, psychic ability and power enhance every aspect of life. A part of every human's nature, it can be ignored . . . or developed and used, reaffirming the psychic nature inherent in every being in the universe.

The following were typical questions we asked Sedona Psychic Seminar participants:

1. What is your reaction to Sedona?

2. Do you feel more psychic here than you normally are?

3. What was your most interesting vortex experience?

Answers to the first question, although diverse, were always positive.

As to feeling more psychic, most people agreed that the vortex energy raises spiritual consciousness and psychic awareness. This was probably best expressed by E.H. of Birmingham, Michigan, who said she felt more psychic "because I'm surrounded by people possessing positive thinking and the desire to search for closer contact with higher consciousness/self," and J.A. of Prescott, Arizona, who answered, "It's easier to achieve an altered state and to receive impressions."

We got a wide range of responses to the third question, including this one from a woman who had been given a "healing weight loss" while in the vortex:

Question 1: "Beautiful!"

Question 2: "Somewhat, but not dramatically. I trust my intuition all the time."

Question 3: "I went to Bell Rock with no particular expectation and started to sit down on a rock when a voice inside my head said, 'Okay, Aquarius, come sit by the water.' There was a small trickle of water coming down a nearby rock, so I sat beside it. Planning to use automatic writing as Dick instructed, in my notebook I wrote, 'Is it important for me to be here?' The answer was instantly in my mind . . . very strong: 'Only for the healing.' This surprised me because I am very healthy, except for being about 50 pounds overweight. As that thought crossed my mind, another strong message came in: 'That is the healing!'

"I then felt some rumblings and unusual movement in my stomach and intestines. When I came down off the rock, everyone was talking about how hungry they were . . . except me. My appetite seems to be cut in half. Whether or not this will last and be a 'cure' remains to be seen. I'll let you know."

B.C.
Palm Springs, California

B.C. did keep us informed. Four weeks after the seminar, she wrote to us, reporting a weight loss of 12 pounds. A month later, she had lost 20 pounds. The next letter, six weeks later, ecstatically told of a weight loss totaling 30 pounds and a new man in her life. And a mailgram, received two months after that, said, "Regret that prior commitments keep me from joining you in Sedona this time. I wanted to strut my new figure and wardrobe, as well as the handsome new man in my life. I have lost 35 pounds since the last Sedona seminar and have gone from a snug size 18 to a loose size 12. My whole life has changed, and it started in Sedona. I'll be there to tell you all the details next time. Thanks a million!"

Question 1: "A spiritual area with lovely vibes."

Question 2: "Perhaps, but it's hard to say. I was led to Sedona and had never heard of Dick Sutphen. Management made all of the arrangements."

Question 3: "At Bell Rock, I heard one high, sharp bell sound. Turning to the east, I communicated with my Indian guide. Turning to the west, I visualized the vortex energy taking shape as a doorway. The energy is not only spiritually uplifting, but physically astounding. Later, we went hiking. I've never hiked in my life and after 12 miles, I felt like I'd only walked a city block!"

E.G.
Alameda, California

Question 1: "This is the most beautiful, serene, psychic place I've ever been. Everyone and everything are just breathtaking!"

Question 2: "I came with my psychic ability really low, but I've been positively upbeat—really have 'tuned-up' psychically, which amazes me!"

Question 3: "While meditating, a beautiful . . . spirit came to me and I felt that he blessed my presence. I picked up a stone and asked the spirits if I could have it. I said, 'If you want me to have it, make it warm.' Nothing happened, so I dropped it and walked further along until I found another stone. This time, it turned hot in my hand!"

A.V.W.
Desert Hot Springs, California

Question 1: "High energy . . . I do not need to eat as much or drink as many fluids here."

Question 2: "Yes! I normally do not experience 'seeing' color, pictures, etc., when I explore psychically."

Question 3: "I'd never tried automatic writing, but Dick convinced me to try it. My first attempt in Boynton Canyon resulted in writings I couldn't read. But when I opened my eyes, I saw a vivid vision. The colors were brilliant and the air seemed to be very thick and 'soupy.' I then received a special message from my own guide.

"As I explained to Dick during a break, I wanted very badly to come to this seminar, but didn't have the money. Not knowing how I'd get it, I put down the deposit to reserve my place. Two days later, one of seven tickets I was holding in the Colorado Lottery turned out to be a $500 winner.

"Upon my arrival in Sedona, I set about looking for a hotel, having made no reservations. I finally found what I was told was the last place in town which included a Saturday night reservation. The only room in town was #7, again my lucky number. Indeed, this has been an eye-opening experience!"

R.G.
Eagle, Colorado

Question 1: "I'm envious of anyone fortunate enough to live here. It is such a vital, invigorating, and beautiful place."

Question 2: "Yes, I really do! The instructions from Dick certainly help. I have seen great results."

Question 3: "In Boynton Canyon, I heard chanting like that on your music tape, 'Crystal Cave.' Then I saw an immense cavern with walls and ceiling of huge crystals. There were figures in meditation postures; they were wearing dark brown robes. They had long gray and white hair."

L.T.L.
Tucson, Arizona

Question 1: "I have experienced an extreme energy that causes tingling sensations on my brow, head area, and hands. The latter is really interesting because my hands are nerve damaged and I normally have no feeling in them at all."

Question 2: "Very definitely so, because I'm generally not psychic at all, but the last few days I've known what Dick, my roommate, and the TV were going to say before they said it."

Question 3: "At Boynton Canyon, when I went into meditation, a deep male voice said, 'Ru Ruid, Ra Rhuim.' I don't have the faintest idea what that means, but my purpose in this life became very clear to me.

"I was told I had cleared most of my karma, except for that with my ex-husband."

R.H.
Yucca Valley, California

Question 1: "Magnificent!"

Question 2: "Visions are more vivid and clearer."

Question 3: "In the vortex, I lay down with my head facing north and with a large crystal on my forehead and a small one on my solar plexus. I then began to meditate.

"First, a vivid emerald green, as if I'd stepped into a green overcast day. I was there and I looked down and saw my feet walking in moccasins and I was wearing fringed leather pants. Then I was running and I saw all the canyons and mesas as if I had lived in the area before. Everything was shaded in green but the views were superb.

"Then everything began to turn purple and violet, and I was running toward a man dressed as a medieval friar. He was half-turned to me, beckoning to me. I ran to him, but a dark mist flowed between us and I couldn't go any further. Something was holding me back. I'm still trying to put this together with the many other experiences I had."

J.C.H.
Lynn, Massachusetts

Question 1: "I am totally in love with it."

Question 2: "Not necessarily, but it encourages it."

Question 3: "At the Airport Mesa Vortex, I had a very strong feeling of peace and perceived a gentle female presence. I then saw The Great Mother weep. She is very tall and slender, and she wears a white dress. Her hair is very long, blows in the wind and the crows play in her hair. The medallion I see upon her breast shines in the sun. It is a sign of the One."

P.C.
Pacifica, California

Question 1: "This is my third 'high' here! Love the energy and group communion."

Question 2: "Yes, since I'm a relative newcomer to metaphysics, I feel I have made great strides the past few days in getting my own self out of the way of my psychic abilities."

Question 3: "Intense vibrations, particularly in my hands."

R.K.
Carlsbad, California

Question 1: "It is a beautiful, peaceful place. I feel it is conducive to 'psychic-ness' for me only because I do not feel the need to protect or close myself off here."

Question 2: "No, I am normally quite empathic, and pick up emotions and physical feelings of others readily. I have random, uncontrolled experiences of knowing things. I work with dreams a lot."

Question 3: "In the Boynton Canyon area, I had a panicked 'crowd' reaction. I felt surrounded by people—all talking to each other and to me at once. It was quite unpleasant. I felt the need to get away, out to wide open spaces. I found a spot where I was alone and sat for a while, but was distracted by a buzzing sound, like the murmur of a huge crowd in the next room.

"Objectively, I know I encountered four people in the hour and a half I was there. They were all quiet and friendly. I have had the panic reaction of feeling enclosed by others' energy repeatedly in the past, but I have always truly been in a crowded place.

"I have three theories: 1) My husband was panicking in a crowd and I picked it up; 2) Many spirits in the area were trying to get my attention and I was unable to focus on one; 3) It doesn't mean anything. I was just paranoid that day."

K.M.F.
Benson, Arizona

Although the reports in this book are very representative of those experienced by the majority of responding seminar participants, all are subjective, and in most cases, different. It would be a mistake to come to Sedona with preconceived expectations. The area appears to be very [connected to the] spiritual and highly charged with energy, resulting in people being more empathic. However, I should point out that there is no guarantee of this.

It is also important to be aware that the Sedona energy seems to intensify your own personal energy, whether positive or negative, and the energy between people. Therefore, your state of being while in Sedona may very well determine how you experience it.

From all accounts, it seems to be a positive and worthwhile experience. The fact that the seminars are almost always filled to capacity (250 plus) even though we schedule them two or three times a year, and that many participants come back again and again, makes me feel that it continues to be a spiritual growth experience.

It is probably best expressed in the participants' own words.

"The seminar was one of the very best events of my life. It came at the end of a five-year period of very unsettling happenings in my life and I was at a point of confusion. The seminar melded all the good things I'd gleaned from the past five years, for I have been searching diligently. Everything came together in a clear, simple picture.

"The seminar was the beginning of my new life. It's almost a month later, and I'm still on my 'Sedona high.' Everything in my life is so much easier now—everything is changing or has changed, and I'm headed in a completely positive direction."

Name Withheld
Topeka, Kansas

"I spent a week in Sedona. My overall energy increased to such an extent that I took action on a work-related situation that had been a problem for years."

J.T.S.
Denver, Colorado

"I thoroughly loved every minute I was there—I loved all the people there, including myself, unconditionally. I loved the area, the energy, and everything about the experience."

D.C.
Burley, Idaho

SEDONA, PSYCHIC ENERGY VORTEXES

"Although I have been concentrating on working on spiritual development for some time now, I have had trouble visualizing and have also had great difficulty trusting my 'mental impressions.' Gradually, since the seminar, I have improved with the trusting.

"During this seminar, I began visualizing more frequently and clearly, and also began being more accurate with information through impression."

F.H.S.
Gaithersburg, Maryland

"It has taken me years to 'trust myself,' but I am beginning to. I believe the meaning of the seminar for me was to listen, and to become motivated to write the book I have been promising to write since the various guides began channeling through me. Why are we so hard to convince? There are so very few persons to whom I would even mention the writings that it is a blessed relief to be part of a high-consciousness gathering, such as you had in Sedona.

"We thank you also for being so down-to-earth about it all. We enjoyed your marvelous sense of humor and lighthearted yet serious approach to the different exercises."

S.M.
Dolan Springs, Arizona

"It brings together people who have trodden the path before. I knew I had to come. I was coming home."

M.P.
Escondido, California

CONCLUSION

During a radio talk show, the host asked me, "Richard, exactly what do you think the Sedona vortexes amount to? How do you explain the experiences people have there?" I responded by saying that after years of exploring in Sedona, I think the vortexes can be summarized as an "energy enhancing field." In other words, the energy emitting from the vortexes intensifies an individual's own energy. So if an individual is interested in tapping into his psychic energies, he will experience an enhancement of those energies while in Sedona. But if an individual comes to Sedona filled with negativity, then his negativity will also become intensified. The vortexes will affect all areas of your life, even the energy between you and someone else. If your relationship is positive, it will probably become more positive while in the area. The same would be true in reverse.

Is there some great crystal buried in Sedona? Maybe, but what does it matter? Is Sedona on ley lines with other great spiritual areas? Sure, but so what? What is important is that your energy is enhanced when you are in the vortexes. Psychic energy, healing energy, love energy, and energy that can be used to go within and find your own answers may be a little easier in the vortexes than elsewhere.

I don't see it as metaphysical or spiritual. The energy is just what is, and it can be explained in very down-to-earth terms. Albert Einstein discovered that matter is energy. A rock appears to be solid, but in reality, it is a mass of vibrating, pulsating molecules. The same is true of plants, animals, and people. We are all energy. Your body is energy. Your mind is energy. Your soul is energy. The only difference between them is their vibrational rate. It may be that when you enter the vortex areas, your vibrational rate is increased. Even a minimal increase in your vibrational rate would enable you to do things and experience things beyond your normal abilities.

I contend we are all here on earth to evolve spiritually. As we evolve, we increase our vibrational rate. Maybe the Sedona vortexes provide us with a preview of our natural abilities a few lifetimes down the evolutionary road.

ENDNOTES

Introduction to the Vortexes

1. Lyall Watson, *The Romeo Error: A Matter of Life and Death* (London: Hodder and Stoughton, 1974), page 170.

2. Heather Hughes, "Religion of the Red Mountains," *Sedona Life* magazine (January 1, 1976).

Chapter 1

1. Hiram C. Hodge, *Arizona As It Was, 1877* (Glorieta, NM: Rio Grande Press, 1965).

Chapter 2

1. Franklin Barnett, *Viola Jimulla: The Indian Chieftess* (Prescott, AZ: Prescott Yavapai Indians, 1967).

2. Sigrid Khera, *The Yavapai of Fort McDowell* (1979).

Chapter 5

1. Charles W. Leadbeater, *The Inner Life* (Wheaton, IL: Quest Books Theosophical Publishing House, 1978), page 14.

2. Ibid, pages 15–16.

BIBLIOGRAPHY

Barnett, Franklin. *Viola Jimulla: The Indian Chieftess*. Prescott, Arizona: Prescott Yavapai Indians, 1968.

Boyd, Sharon. "Healing Power of Sedona," *Master of Life*, issue 43, n.d.

———. "Sedona: The Path of the Heart," *Master of Life*, issue 45, n.d.

———. "The Vortex Revisited." *Self-Help Update,* issue 21, n.d.

Hodge, Hiram C. *1877 Arizona As It Was*. Glorieta, New Mexico: Rio Grande Press, Inc., 1965. First published 1877 as *Arizona As It Is* by Hurd and Houghton (New York); H.O. Houghton and Company (Boston).

Harrison, Mike and John Williams. *Oral History of the Yavapai*, ed. Sigrid Khera, Ph.D. and Carolina C. Butler. Tucson, Arizona: The University of Arizona Press, 2015. First published 1979 as *The Yavapai of Fort McDowell* by Fort McDowell Indian Community (Fountain Hills, Arizona). Citations refer to the 1979 edition.

Schnebly, Ellsworth M. "How Sedona Was Named," *Those Early Days. Oldtimers' Memoirs*. Sedona, Arizona: Sedona Westerners, 1975.

Thompson, Albert E. "The Story of Sedona," *Those Early Days. Oldtimers' Memoirs*. Sedona, Arizona: Sedona Westerners, 1975.

ABOUT THE AUTHOR

Dick Sutphen (1937–2020) was an author, hypnotist, and seminar trainer. He developed innovative group hypnosis exploration techniques that are now being used internationally. His best-selling books *You Were Born Again to Be Together; Past Lives, Future Loves;* and *Unseen Influences* have become classic metaphysical/self-help titles.

Dick appeared on many TV shows, such as *Good Morning America*. In 1976, he conducted the first nationally broadcast past-life regression on Tom Snyder's NBC show *Tomorrow*. A 90-minute *David Susskind Show* was built around Dick's work and is still being rerun years later as one of the series' most popular programs. He appeared on over 350 radio and television shows.

Dick was the author of over 32 books and more than 600 hypnosis, meditation, and regressive hypnosis audio programs. He had a 50-year background in psychic investigation and human-potential exploration that includes being the founder and former director of a hypnosis center in Scottsdale, Arizona. He is survived by his wife, Roberta.

For more information visit dicksutphen.com or write to info@dicksutphen.com.

BONUS CONTENT

Thank you for purchasing *Sedona, Psychic Energy Vortexes* by
Dick Sutphen. This product includes free downloads! To access
this bonus content, please visit www.hayhouse.com/download
and enter the Product ID and Download Code
as they appear below.

For the free audio meditations, enter:
Product ID: 6829
Download Code: audio

For the free automatic writing course, enter:
Product ID: 6829
Download Code: course

For further assistance, please contact Hay House Customer Care
by phone: US (800) 654-5126 or INTL CC+(760) 431-7695 or visit
www.hayhouse.com/contact.

Thank you again for your Hay House purchase. Enjoy!
Hay House, Inc. • P.O. Box 5100 • Carlsbad, CA 92018
(800) 654-5126

Caution: This audio program features meditation/visualization exercises that
render it inappropriate for use while driving or operating heavy machinery.

Publisher's note: Hay House products are intended to be powerful, inspira-
tional, and life-changing tools for personal growth and healing. They are not
intended as a substitute for medical care. Please use this audio program under
the supervision of your care provider. Neither the author nor Hay House,
Inc., assumes any responsibility for your improper use of this product.

Hay House Titles of Related Interest

YOU CAN HEAL YOUR LIFE, the movie,
starring Louise Hay & Friends
(available as an online streaming video)
www.hayhouse.com/louise-movie

THE SHIFT, the movie,
starring Dr. Wayne W. Dyer
(available as an online streaming video)
www.hayhouse.com/the-shift-movie

*BECOMING SUPERNATURAL: How Common People
Are Doing the Uncommon,* by Dr. Joe Dispenza

*THE MAP OF CONSCIOUSNESS EXPLAINED:
A Proven Energy Scale to Actualize Your Ultimate Potential,*
by David R. Hawkins, M.D., Ph.D.

*MESSAGES FROM SPIRIT: The Extraordinary Power of Oracles,
Omens, and Signs,* by Colette Baron-Reid

*THE VORTEX: Where the Law of Attraction Assembles All
Cooperative Relationships,* by Esther and Jerry Hicks

All of the above are available at your local bookstore,
or may be ordered by contacting Hay House (see next page).

We hope you enjoyed this Hay House book. If you'd like to receive our online catalog featuring additional information on Hay House books and products, or if you'd like to find out more about the Hay Foundation, please contact:

Hay House, Inc., P.O. Box 5100, Carlsbad, CA 92018-5100
(760) 431-7695 or (800) 654-5126
(760) 431-6948 (fax) or (800) 650-5115 (fax)
www.hayhouse.com® • www.hayfoundation.org

Published in Australia by: Hay House Australia Pty. Ltd.,
18/36 Ralph St., Alexandria NSW 2015
Phone: 612-9669-4299 • *Fax:* 612-9669-4144
www.hayhouse.com.au

Published in the United Kingdom by: Hay House UK, Ltd.,
The Sixth Floor, Watson House, 54 Baker Street, London W1U 7BU
Phone: +44 (0)20 3927 7290 • *Fax:* +44 (0)20 3927 7291
www.hayhouse.co.uk

Published in India by: Hay House Publishers India,
Muskaan Complex, Plot No. 3, B-2, Vasant Kunj, New Delhi 110 070
Phone: 91-11-4176-1620 • *Fax:* 91-11-4176-1630
www.hayhouse.co.in

Access New Knowledge.
Anytime. Anywhere.

Learn and evolve at your own pace
with the world's leading experts.

www.hayhouseU.com